M Y FRIEND ANNE BARBOUR has written some powerful songs like the "Lion and the Lamb," and
"The Light of that City" (written with her husband John
Barbour). She now has written a devotional titled *Jesus |
Love to the End*, focusing on the greatest moment of all
time: the Cross, and the Resurrection of the Lord Jesus
Christ. Her insights based on Scripture leading up to
the Easter story will shine the light on the Savior of the
world and the eternal life He offers to all who will follow
Him in obedience all the way to Heaven.

— FRANKLIN GRAHAM
President and CEO, Samaritan's Purse
Billy Graham Evangelical Association

JESUS

LOVE *to* THE END

JESUS
LOVE to THE END

A Devotional to
Prepare Your Heart For Easter

ANNE BARBOUR

FAITH
HAPPENINGS
PUBLISHERS

CENTENNIAL, COLO.

FaithHappenings Publishing
A division of WordServe Literary
7500 E. Arapahoe Rd., Suite 285 • Centennial, CO 80112
admin@wordserveliterary.com • 303.471.6675

Cover Design: Francine Eden Platt • Eden Graphics, Inc.
Cover Photo: Sharon McCutcheon
Interior Book Design: Francine Eden Platt • Eden Graphics, Inc.
Interior Photos: stock.adobe.com and istockphoto.com
Bio Photo: Nina Russo Photography

ISBN: 978-1-941555-52-1

First Printing, February 2022

~ For Mom and Dad ~

Your passion for our Savior
shaped your little girl's heart
so that I too am
deeply in love with Jesus.
Thank you both for showing me the way!

Love, Anne

Introduction

Dear Reader,

WHATEVER TRADITIONS and practices make up your preparation for Easter each year, the focus—the point of it all—is Jesus. You are about to spend the next forty days preparing your heart and saturating yourself in the narrative of the final weeks of Jesus' life before His death and resurrection. I believe you will come away with a deeper awareness, not that Jesus is central in the story, but rather that He is the sum total of the story.

For some Christians, the weeks leading up to Easter are referred to as "Lent" and involve practices such as fasting and self-denial. The point is to identify with Jesus' days of deprivation when He was tempted in the desert as well as His suffering in the days leading up to and through His death. The family of faith I grew up in did not integrate such practices into our church life. We did, however, practice weekly Communion as a church family. I was immersed in the scenes and stories surrounding Jesus' death, burial, and resurrection with such frequency that when Easter came 'round each spring, I was thrilled to have arrived at the pinnacle of celebration for Christ followers. Those formative years provided a unique segue into the writing of this devotional and my personal spiritual focus in the weeks leading up to Easter. Now, I greatly anticipate these forty days, knowing I will meet with Jesus in a way unique to any other period of the year.

As I explored traditions including Lent, I was confronted with the temptation to construct a template that would emphasize the Christ Follower rather than The Christ. I recognized that at the close of forty days, I could end up having done too much thinking about what I "gave up" through fasting and how pleased the Lord would be in response to my intentionality. The Spirit spoke clearly and firmly to my heart—this endeavor would be about Jesus, and Jesus alone. As I wrote, with Him walking me through the gospel accounts, there was no trouble whatsoever coming into alignment with Him.

I have borrowed the start and finish line, and the possibility of fasting from the Lent tradition, but even those two things are tied loosely to this devotional. Most importantly, my intention is that you would slip into different scenes in the latter days of the life of Jesus and experience Him and His actions as if you were there. While much of what you will read and ponder comes chronologically, this devotional is a thematic journey, experiential in nature. It should not be viewed as a discipline or practice, but rather as an opportunity to intentionally pursue the person of Jesus as He is revealed in the details of His story.

May the Spirit of God use this devotional to lead you into the presence of the Risen Savior. I pray that having encountered Him, you will be content to linger with Him for forty days. I pray that through your experience of Him, you will never be the same, nor will your worship of Him be the same. And I pray that a fire will ignite within you with an irrepressible eagerness to express your gratitude, love, and adoration for Jesus, who sacrificed His life that you might live.

With Prayer and Great Expectation,

Anne Barbour

Now before the Feast of the Passover
when Jesus knew that His hour had come
to depart out of this world to the Father,
having loved His own who were in the world,
He loved them to the end.

~ JOHN 13:1 (ESV)

GUIDE to reading
Jesus | Love to the End

WELCOME TO *Jesus | Love to the End – A Devotional to Prepare Your Heart for Easter.* Beginning on Ash Wednesday, you will find an entry for each day through Easter Eve. You will notice that there are no entries for any of the Sundays that fall during this period. Sundays are days of rest set aside for you to be with your family of faith and engage in your usual practices in prayer and in the Word of God. Here is a short guide to help you get the most out of this devotional.

Meditation:

These passages from the Bible are here for reflection, providing opportunities for the Lord to give you a fresh look at pieces of the story surrounding Jesus' final weeks on the earth. I encourage you to linger in the passages, allowing your soul to settle in the presence of God. There is so much treasure to be found for those who will wait upon Him in this way, especially if the passages of scripture are very familiar.

Reflection:

This section provides reflections from the daily passage. They are meant to ignite streams of thought as you remain in the presence of the Lord. This practice of listening to the Holy Spirit is not always easy, but it is where the treasure is, so as much as you are able, don't be in a hurry. Practice listening as you go about your daily activities. So often the Holy Spirit will use a real-life moment to give deeper meaning to the passages and reflections you've just read.

Response:

The prayer provided is a launchpad into your own dialogue with God. I would encourage you to ask God to speak to you as you move through the business of your day. Enjoy His presence with you each day as you remember who He is and the significance of His life, death, and resurrection from the dead.

Remember:

This section provides you with an opportunity to jot down thoughts as you meditate, and reflect, and pray. In doing so you create a time capsule for the future which I pray will make this volume especially meaningful in the years to come. There are so many benefits to remembering how the Lord stirred our hearts and what it is He meant for us to pay attention to on a particular occasion.

TABLE OF CONTENTS

In Preparation

Meditation:

I will instruct you and teach you
in the way you should go;
I will counsel you with My eye upon you.

~ PSALM 32:8

For thus says the One who is high and lifted up,
who inhabits eternity, whose name is Holy:
"I dwell in the high and holy place, and also
with him who is of a contrite and lowly spirit."

~ ISAIAH 57:15

Reflection:

Today is Ash Wednesday, the first day of our journey, and we embark on a path that will carry us through the day preceding Easter Sunday. I am asking the Lord if He would give each of us an experience of Himself that will make these weeks especially meaningful, one that will bring true soul change, marked by an increased eagerness to glorify the Risen Savior of the world. In preparation, we prayerfully consider whether there is a sacrifice that would be appropriate for us to make during these weeks.

Fasting and the forgoing of certain luxuries is a traditional part of Lent sometimes referred to as the Lenten Sacrifice. It's generally seen as a point of identification with the forty days Jesus spent in the desert. Our forefathers as early as 325A.D. began to form and practice a version of what we now embrace as tradition. Our purpose, however, is quite simple. Eliminating an activity creates space that we set aside to be with the Lord. Creating an appetite through fasting provides a chance to feast on the words of Jesus and on communion with Him.

One of the cautions I feel quite strongly as I consider what I might forgo is that I not mistake a few temporary sacrifices as having spiritual benefit in and of themselves. It is the Holy Spirit within me who does the work of enlightenment and growth through my cooperation with Him. In other words, we will purpose NOT to focus on what we are temporarily going without, but on intentionally moving toward Jesus and moving *with* Him toward the remembrance of His crucifixion and resurrection from the dead. How else could God possibly be honored in the coming weeks as He ought to be? I have an idea that's what our forefathers had in mind in the first place.

Secondly, in case there would be any inkling within us temping us to elevate ourselves for the "grand sacrifice" we are about make, let's remember "All that is in the heavens and on the earth is Yours" (1 Chronicles 29:11). In light of this very important truth, it's going to be difficult (in a good way) to feel self-righteous or sorry for ourselves for whatever the Lord might ask us to lay aside. We might have to remind each other of that along the way!

So, what will you and I fast? What will we lay aside so that we create space to allow the Spirit of God to prepare us to rightly honor Him at Easter? I believe the Lord will happily speak to us about what He would have us forgo, reminding us that the objective is to find our way into His presence, cooperative and expectant. He will do the rest.

Response:

Lord Jesus,

I come to You and ask, what would you have me lay aside in these weeks preceding Easter? What in my life might be keeping me from making space for You? Where have I, intentionally or otherwise, cluttered my daily schedule so that I find little room for drawing away with You? Speak to me. Show me what You would have me do, and I will do it. And thank You for the will and the strength to cooperate with You. Glorify Yourself through my life as never before because of this time we will spend together! ~*Amen*

Remember:

CONSIDER HIM

Meditation:

Therefore, since we are surrounded
by so great a cloud of witnesses,
let us also lay aside every weight,
and sin which clings so closely,
and let us run with endurance
the race that is set before us,
looking to Jesus, the founder
and perfecter of our faith,
who for the joy that was set
before Him endured the cross,
despising the shame, and is seated
at the right hand of the throne of God.
Consider Him who endured from sinners
such hostility against Himself, so that
you may not grow weary or fainthearted.

~ HEBREWS 12:1—3

Reflection:

Why are we encouraged by the writer of Hebrews to "consider Him?" Why "look to Jesus?" If you and I are going to "run" through the next several weeks with endurance, it's going to come as we look to Jesus. He is the reason we will not grow fainthearted. And if we are truly going to "consider Him," we are going to have to let Him slow the train of our lives down. And so, we fast certain activities to create space, and certain foods to create an appetite. The space and the appetite opened within us are for Him to fill.

I encourage you to read each day's meditation and "consider" Jesus. Ask the Holy Spirit to show Him to you. He lives in you to do that very thing. He wants to teach you and reveal the beauty and majesty of Jesus to you. The Spirit of God invites you to linger with Him—to meditate on the Word of God because there is treasure waiting for you if you will.

If you are not accustomed to reading the Bible like this, ask the Lord to help you. He will. You can open the Word of God, expecting Him to be your personal guide and teacher. He will speak as you meditate on the words in each day's passage of Scripture. Use the Remember section to record what you hear Him say. This will become a written testament of your personal journey with the Lord. It's a time capsule that will come to reflect this particular Easter season.

As you close this book each day and go about your business, ask the Lord to help you ruminate on what He's said to you. Ask Him to keep speaking to you so that even while you are busy about your life, you are aware of Him, hearing His voice, and enjoying His nearness.

Response:

Lord Jesus,

Today I want to saturate my mind with thoughts of You. I want to engage with You. I want to hear from You and talk to You. I long to grow so accustomed to Your voice, no amount of noise can keep me from hearing You when You speak. Please help me to steward the space I'm opening through setting aside certain activities. Help me to feast on Your Word and be satisfied as if I were eating the most luxurious food. Help me to consider You and to look to You. Be glorified through me today, Lord. ~*Amen*

Remember:

_____

_____

_____

_____

_____

_____

_____

_____

_____

_____

Humble My Heart

Meditation:

And He humbled you and let you hunger
and fed you with manna, which you did not know,
nor did your fathers know, that He might make
you know that man does not live by bread alone,
but man lives by every word that comes
from the mouth of the Lord.

~ DEUTERONOMY 8:3

Good and upright is the Lord;
therefore He instructs sinners in the way.
He leads the humble in what is right,
and teaches the humble His way. All the paths
of the Lord are steadfast love and faithfulness, for
those who keep His covenant and His testimonies.

~ PSALM 25:8–10

Clothe yourselves, all of you,
with humility toward one another,
for "God opposes the proud
but gives grace to the humble."

~ 1 PETER 5:5

Reflection:

We are "considering" Jesus. We are looking to Him, the founder and perfector of our faith. Now, in His presence, we examine the condition of our heart. For us to be able to receive from Him freely, we must be people contrite and humble. If we move into the forthcoming narrative of

Jesus' life proudly, we will never be able to be influenced by His voice. After all, He teaches the humble His way.

Jesus knows the content of a person's heart. And *only* He knows the deepest motivations that explain why we do the things we do. So, He must be the one to bring illumination. We are not capable of honestly assessing our own hearts. If we purpose to meditate on the passages in this entry, and if we ask Him to quiet our hearts and open our ears to hear His voice, I know He will speak to us.

Should the Lord shine a light on an area of darkness within us, we can be fully confident that He will give us the strength to not only look upon that newly lit place, but also to take any necessary action. Some of us will be prompted to go to someone in our life with whom we are in conflict and initiate resolution. Some of us will be exposed to pride in our hearts. That will have to be submitted to Jesus. All of us must be willing to ask that God would make any adjustments necessary to humble our hearts.

Humble followers of Jesus are not fighting with Him for lordship. They understand that the only path to thriving is when the child of God is submitted, eager for Jesus to be Lord of the breadth of their life. He *is* Lord. He purchased us for Himself because He deeply longs for us to have uninhibited access to His presence. In His presence, we find a companionship richer than we will ever be able to comprehend. The path to such riches requires the humbling of our hearts. It is a price so negligible compared to the treasure to be found in communion with Him. May we run to Him unhesitatingly and bow in full submission.

Response:

Lord Jesus,

Please humble my heart. Do whatever is needed so that I am in a position to receive from You fully. You know my inmost parts. You created me. You know me far better than I will ever know myself. I trust You to humble my heart and I'm also afraid for that to happen. Help me to release my fears. They are unwarranted. My head knows that but my heart is stubborn and willful. You hate pride more than anything. Do what You have to do to kill it in me! I open my heart to You. Be glorified through me, Lord. Thank You! ~*Amen*

Remember:

_____

_____

_____

_____

_____

_____

_____

_____

OF YOUR OWN
WE HAVE GIVEN YOU

Meditation:

Yours, O Lord, is the greatness and the
power and the glory and the victory and
the majesty, for all that is in the heavens
and in the earth is Yours.
Yours is the kingdom, O Lord,
and You are exalted as head above all.
Both riches and honor come from You,
and You rule over all.
In Your hand are power and might,
and in Your hand it is to make great
and to give strength to all.
And now we thank You, our God,
and praise Your glorious name.
But who am I, and what is my people,
that we should be able thus to offer willingly?
For all things come from You,
and of Your own have we given You.

~ 1 CHRONICLES 29:11-14

Reflection:

This is the final foundational thought before we enter the
narrative of the last days of Jesus' life before His death and
resurrection. As I write, I cannot escape this passage written
by King David. It has been and remains very important

in my personal annual pilgrimage to Easter. Simply stated, all I have is the Lord's. Every relationship, every belonging, every talent and gift I have, every opportunity I have to exercise those gifts—the full sum of my resources, both tangible and intangible, including my own mind and soul and body, belong to the Lord. Which means they do not belong to me. I steward them. Even when I function as though they belong to me, I am still only and ever stewarding.

And that means that more times than I could count, I have acted the fool, believing I am bestowing some grand gift upon the Lord through my fasting, when in reality, I am simply putting on pause something that's His in the first place. I uncover my slothfulness as I make space for the Lord through fasting. Why isn't that space protected for Him in the first place? And that He should have to humble my heart reveals yet another blunder in my understanding of what belongs to whom. Where is there ever space for pride in the heart of a person who is entirely indebted to the One who saved her—who "bought" her with His blood?

King David understood there is nothing we will ever give, offer, or sacrifice that is anything other than the return of something entrusted to us. And he saw the giving back of it as a sacred privilege. I'm certain we are to think about our fasting, the setting aside of time for Him, and being delivered from pridefulness, in the same light.

The day of our Lord's crucifixion is commemorated nearly four weeks from today. Perhaps the greatest gift He could give us is a deeper experience of Himself so that our appetites hunger for Him more than for our creature comforts. We will ask him for this as we pray today. In the meantime, it's good to remember: "But who am I, and what is my people, that we should be able thus to offer willingly?"

Response:

Lord Jesus,

You are the great gift giver. All that I have is from You including those things that You have asked me to lay aside for these weeks. Help me, by Your Spirit, to be grateful in the giving and not resentful or entitled. Turn my eyes to You and away from myself and the trappings of life. And now, Jesus, keep my gaze fixed upon You. Meet me today and in the weeks ahead and talk to me about Yourself—about Your beautiful life, about Your death and resurrection, and about the HOPE for humankind (for me) that arose because of all You accomplished! Thank You! Be glorified! ~*Amen*

Remember:

_____

_____

_____

_____

_____

_____

Sunday
Day of Rest

JESUS, IN THE DESERT

Meditation:

"And you shall remember the whole way that the Lord
your God has led you these forty years in the wilderness,
that He might humble you, testing you to know what was in
your heart, whether you would keep His commandments or
not. And He humbled you and let you hunger and fed you
with manna, which you did not know, nor did your fathers
know, that He might make you know that man does
not live by bread alone, but man lives by every
word that comes from the mouth of the Lord."

~ DEUTERONOMY 8:2–3

In those days Jesus came from Nazareth of Galilee
and was baptized by John in the Jordan. And when
He came up out of the water, immediately He saw the
heavens being torn open and the Spirit descending
on Him like a dove. And a voice came from heaven,
"You are my beloved Son; with you I am well pleased."

The Spirit immediately drove Him out into the
wilderness. And He was in the wilderness forty days,
being tempted by Satan. And the tempter came and said to
Him, "If You are the Son of God, command these
stones to become loaves of bread." But He answered,
"It is written, "'Man shall not live by bread alone, but
by every word that comes from the mouth of God.'"

~ MARK 1:9–13; MATTHEW 4:3–4

Reflection:

It's time to jump into the narrative of Jesus' public life. This first milestone we look at is the final step in launching the public ministry of Jesus. The passages you just read are familiar enough to many of us to miss some of the key elements that make up what happens to Jesus and who is involved. Take as much time as you need with the Lord and ask Him to put you in the story with Him. Ask Him to show you things you have not seen before.

God leads His children into the desert for forty years. God leads Jesus into the desert for forty days. Both scenarios are humbling and difficult, stripping away fundamental necessities like food and water. Both leave the temporary desert dwellers very vulnerable, at the mercy of God for life-giving provision. One is a test to see what is in the heart of the people of God. The other gives Satan access to the Son of Man "until the devil had ended every temptation" (Luke 4:13). And both highlight the reality that what ultimately sustains a person is every word that comes from the mouth of God.

Jesus is victorious in the desert where the children of God seldom are. They choose to chafe against God and complain, resenting Him for the hardship of the desert experience. In contrast, Jesus is compliant and submitted. He does not resist suffering, but instead embraces the One who is providing for Him in it. Jesus enters the desert "full of the Holy Spirit" (Luke 4:1), and He departs "full of the power of the Spirit" (Luke 4:14).

We likely have no trouble identifying with the children of Israel in response to hardship. So Jesus' obedience and cooperation under dire conditions is meant to show us what's possible despite our fleshly tendencies! Throughout today (especially while we have the remembrance of the crucifixion and resurrection in our sights), let's pull on the coattails of the Holy Spirit, asking Him to speak to us about Jesus' time in the desert. What can we learn about Jesus in His humanity? How did He practice trust? What does He want us to know about Himself through this look into His days in the desert?

Response:

Lord Jesus,

There are a lifetime of lessons in the story of You in the desert. What is it You would say as I meditate and listen? Forty days of being tempted, and in such an unforgiving environment, leaves me wondering why this was allowed to happen in the first place. But You remind me constantly— You don't think like I do, and Your ways are not my ways. Please meet with me now and tell me what You want me to know. ~*Amen*

Remember:

_____

_____

_____

_____

_____

DRIVEN BY THE HOLY SPIRIT

Meditation:

And he [John the Baptist] preached, saying,
"After me comes He who is mightier than I,
the strap of whose sandals I am not
worthy to stoop down and untie.
I have baptized you with water, but
He will baptize you with the Holy Spirit."

~ MARK 1: 7–8

And I will give you a new heart,
and a new spirit I will put within you.
And I will remove the heart of stone from
your flesh and give you a heart of flesh.
And I will put my Spirit within you,
and cause you to walk in my statutes
and be careful to obey my rules.

~ EZEKIEL 36:26–27

He saw the heavens being torn open and
the Spirit descending on Him like a dove.
The Spirit immediately drove Him
out into the wilderness.

~ MARK 1:10, 12

Reflection:

Is Jesus driven by the Holy Spirit? Once the Spirit comes upon Him at His baptism, we find Jesus empowered and under the direction of God the Holy Spirit. The first act of the Holy Spirit after having descended upon Jesus is to drive Him to the desert for forty arduous days of hardship and testing by Satan.

That seems like a strange act for a member of the Godhead to inflict upon another member of the Godhead. We might prefer to think of the Spirit of God as the Comforter, and He is that. But He is also the one who directs us and shapes us so that we look more like the One we are fashioned after. Jesus willingly subjects Himself to the Holy Spirit and the desert experience. This trial is used as part of a thirty-year "shaping" that will prepare Jesus for the public ministry ahead of Him.

Why consider this during our approach to Easter? We, too, as Christ Ones, are descended upon by the Holy Spirit at the time of our salvation. So we can learn from the active presence of the Spirit in the life of our Savior. We can learn from Jesus what it looks like to be under the power and control of the Spirit of God. While we can see the Spirit challenging Jesus in incomprehensible ways, we can also see that same Spirit providing counsel and comfort, resourcing Jesus every time He is in need.

The role of the Holy Spirit in Jesus' three-year public ministry is likely far greater than we can ever understand. As we move forward into the narrative, let's ask the Lord to help us keep a lookout for the work of the Spirit in the life of Jesus in this final season of His life on the earth. It will give us insight into the role the Spirit means to play in our own lives.

Response:

Lord Jesus,

The Spirit was upon You and guided You. Speak to me about the relationship You shared with Him, especially from the time He drove You into the desert. He was a key Person for You, I know. You have shared Your essence with Him from eternity, but during these last years of Your earthly life, the interaction You had with the Spirit seems unique. Teach me. And thank You for giving me a glimpse into the life the Holy Spirit means to have within me. Thank You once again for showing the path to thriving in relationship with Father, Son, and Spirit. ~*Amen*

Remember:

The Ways of Jesus

Meditation:

Love your enemies, do good to those who hate you,
bless those who curse you, pray for those who abuse you.
To one who strikes you on the cheek, offer the
other also, and from one who takes away your
cloak do not withhold your tunic either.

Give to everyone who begs from you,
and from one who takes away your goods
do not demand them back.

And as you wish that others would do to you,
do so to them. If you love those who love you,
what benefit is that to you?

For even sinners love those who love them.
And if you do good to those who do good to you,
what benefit is that to you? For even sinners do
the same. And if you lend to those from whom
you expect to receive, what credit is that to you?
Even sinners lend to sinners, to get
back the same amount.

But love your enemies, and do good,
and lend, expecting nothing in return,
and your reward will be great, and you will
be sons of the Most High, for He is kind
to the ungrateful and the evil. Be merciful,
even as your Father is merciful.

~ LUKE 6:27-36

Reflection:

This is the seventh day of our journey, and our attention turns to the seemingly radical values that Jesus holds. I say *seemingly* because I believe God is showing us through the life of Jesus the way He intends for all of us to live. That it appears radical reveals humanity's propensity to establish values that fly in the face of the ways of God. I have an idea that rather than God saying, "Hey, want a radically fresh approach to living your life?" He might say, "Hey, want to know what I've always had in mind for you?"

I'm pretty sure we are the radicals in need of retiring our rogue tendencies so we can embrace the ways of Jesus. In doing so, we will align ourselves with the counter-cultural way Jesus lives while He walks the earth. We'll be living in right relationship with creation, with one another, and with God even while we wait for the redemption that's coming when Jesus returns. There is something very comforting about the idea of falling in step with God and living a normal life as God defines it.

What does God's normal look like? Jesus lives it out. He does not have a different set of values for different life scenarios. All the way up and through His arrest, death, and resurrection, He remains true to the ways of God, NO variation at all. He faces every kind of opposition and hardship you and I face (and immeasurably more), and He responds to them all without compromise. He does this the way He intends for us to do it—by the power of the Spirit of God. Let's turn our attention now to the passage from Luke written above and ask the Lord to speak as we meditate on the ways of Jesus.

Response:

Lord Jesus,

Your ways are NOT my ways: "For My thoughts are not your thoughts, neither are your ways My ways, declares the Lord" (Isaiah 55:8). I'm sorry that keeps surprising me, but it does. So, when I read Your quoted words, I can't help but think how radical You were. In reality, You were simply clarifying the way You have always intended for me to live my life. I feel like I'm being invited to come home, where I've always belonged. Please speak to me today about the beauty of Your ways. Work them into me by Your Spirit!
~ *Amen*

Remember:

_____

_____

_____

_____

_____

_____

_____

Resurrection Power

Meditation:

Soon afterward He [Jesus] went to a town called Nain,
and His disciples and a great crowd went with Him.
As He drew near to the gate of the town, behold,
a man who had died was being carried out, the only
son of his mother, and she was a widow, and
a considerable crowd from the town was with her.
And when the Lord saw her, He had compassion
on her and said to her, "Do not weep."
Then He came up and touched the bier,
and the bearers stood still. And He said,
"Young man, I say to you, arise."
And the dead man sat up and began to
speak, and Jesus gave him to his mother.

~ LUKE 7:11–15

While He was still speaking, someone
from the ruler's house came and said,
"Your daughter is dead; do not
trouble the Teacher any more."
But Jesus on hearing this answered him,
"Do not fear; only believe, and she will be well."
And when He came to the house,
He allowed no one to enter with Him,
except Peter and John and James,
and the father and mother of the child.
And all were weeping and mourning for her,

but He said, "Do not weep, for she is not dead but sleeping."
And they laughed at Him, knowing that she was dead.
But taking her by the hand He called, saying, "Child, arise."
And her spirit returned, and she got up at once.
And He directed that something should be given her to eat.
And her parents were amazed, but He charged
them to tell no one what had happened.

~ LUKE 8:49–56

Martha said to Jesus, "Lord, if you had
been here, my brother would not have died.
But even now I know that whatever
You ask from God, God will give You."
Jesus said to her, "Your brother will rise again."
Martha said to him, "I know that he will rise
again in the resurrection on the last day."
Jesus said to her, "I am the resurrection and the life.
Whoever believes in Me, though he die, yet shall he live,
and everyone who lives and believes in Me shall never die."

~ JOHN 11:21–26

Reflection:

Jesus, under the direction of God the Father and empowered by God the Spirit, exercises His ability to bring dead
people back to life. Jesus has resurrection power, even before He is in possession of His own resurrected body. He
brings the full power of the Godhead to bear in these three
amazing death-to-life stories. Even before He completes
His earthly mission, He demonstrates His altogether otherness, having the power of life over death.

The Savior is nearing the time He will be betrayed and murdered. All the while, He possesses unlimited power so that even death is within His ability to overturn. We can't forget this fact because it keeps us mindful that Jesus' journey to the cross is one He chooses of His own free will, elevating the will of the Father over any ability He has to effect change to His own advantage.

You and I are indwelt by the same Spirit of God that Jesus was. How are you feeling during your fast? How are you doing having set aside a habit? Are you struggling? That struggle is an open door, a unique and favorable opportunity to reach higher than we otherwise might. It gives us a chance to practice elevating the will of the Father over our own will. It also reminds us that the power of God within us can aid us to accomplish absolutely anything the Lord will ask us to do.

Response:

Lord Jesus,

You are God the Son, possessing the fulness of the power of God within You! Praise You, all powerful God! You have shown me what it looks like to prefer the will of the Father, forgoing Your own comfort. You raised people from the dead, yet You did not bring that power to bear on Your own behalf. You had another agenda, handed to You by Your Father. I want to be about His agenda for my life, like You were. Thank You for showing me it can be done by the power of God the Spirit. All praise is Yours! ~*Amen*

Remember:

_____

_____

_____

_____

_____

_____

_____

_____

_____

_____

COMING TO JERUSALEM

Meditation:

The next day the large crowd that had come to
the feast heard that Jesus was coming to Jerusalem.
So they took branches of palm trees and went
out to meet Him, crying out, "Hosanna! Blessed
is He who comes in the name of the Lord,
even the King of Israel!"

And Jesus found a young donkey and sat on it,
just as it is written, "Fear not, daughter of Zion;
behold, your king is coming, sitting on a donkey's colt!"
His disciples did not understand these things at first,
but when Jesus was glorified, then they remembered
that these things had been written about Him
and had been done to Him.

~ JOHN 12:12–16

And when He drew near and saw the city, He wept
over it, saying, "Would that you, even you, had
known on this daythe things that make for peace!
But now they are hidden from your eyes.
For the days will come upon you, when your enemies
will set up a barricade around you and surround
you and hem you in on every side and tear you down
to the ground, you and your children within you.
And they will not leave one stone upon another in you,
because you did not know the time of your visitation."

~ LUKE 19:41–44

And He entered Jerusalem and went into
the temple. And when He had looked
around at everything, as it was already late,
He went out to Bethany with the twelve.

~ MARK 11:11

Reflection:

Before Jesus sets foot in Jerusalem, He is grieving over her. He utters clear foreboding words that express His grief. He is alone in His grief this day because no one but Jesus knows what's coming in the days and decades ahead. The scene is especially lonely as the cheers of the people ring out motivated by the false hope that Jesus is about to become their earthly king.

No one has a grasp of reality—not the crowds, not the plotters, not the disciples, not the merchants trading on the temple floor—not a single other soul understands what's really happening. No one in the natural world is able to share in Jesus' grief.

The isolation our Savior would have lived with throughout His ministry must have been its own source of sorrow. This day highlights it as well as any other. And it's worth noting that while Jesus knows salvation is at hand, He is aware that most throughout the coming ages will not embrace the gift He is about to set before them. So He weeps.

The day finishes with a thorough walk-through of the temple. The condition of it will be addressed tomorrow. In the meantime, Jesus must suffer the weight of what He observes. How heavy His heart must be as He retires to His friends for the night.

Response:

Lord Jesus,

Honestly, this scene breaks my heart. I'm heartbroken for You, enduring the cluelessness of those You were in the company of that day. I confess, I would have been among them. I'm sorry for our cluelessness, Lord. I'm sorry for Your grief. I'm sorry You bore it without the comfort of another human being.

I am undone by Your enduring love for humanity. A day like the one described in these passages reminds me that the quality of Your love is entirely beyond my comprehension. I praise You for Your love. I bow before You, good and patient and merciful One! There is no one like You. Take a thorough walk through the temple of my heart and tell me what You see. I want to be enlightened. I don't want to be standing in Your presence clueless today. I want gratitude to pour forth toward You like a rushing river. Please, Lord, by the power of Your Spirit, glorify Yourself in my life today.
~*Amen*

Remember:

_____

_____

_____

_____

_____

TEMPLE BUSINESS

Meditation:

On the following day, when they came
from Bethany, He was hungry.
And seeing in the distance a fig tree in leaf,
He went to see if He could find anything on it.
When He came to it, He found nothing but
leaves, for it was not the season for figs.
And He said to it, "May no one ever eat fruit
from you again." And His disciples heard it.

And they came to Jerusalem. And He entered
the temple and began to drive out those who
sold and those who bought in the temple, and
He overturned the tables of the money-changers
and the seats of those who sold pigeons.
And He would not allow anyone to carry
anything through the temple.
And He was teaching them and saying to
them, "Is it not written, 'My house shall be
called a house of prayer for all the nations?'
But you have made it a den of robbers."

~ MARK 11:12–17

And the blind and the lame came to Him in the temple,
and He healed them. But when the chief priests and the
scribes saw the wonderful things that He did, and the children crying out in the temple, "Hosanna to the Son
of David!" they were indignant, and they said to Him,

"Do you hear what these are saying?"
And Jesus said to them, "Yes; have you never read,
'Out of the mouth of infants and nursing
babies you have prepared praise'?"

~ MATTHEW 21:14-16

And the chief priests and the scribes heard it
and were seeking a way to destroy Him,
for they feared Him, because all the crowd
was astonished at His teaching. And when
evening came they went out of the city.

~ MARK 11:18-19

Reflection:

This day in the narrative begins with our Savior hungry and a fig tree that's all show and no substance. What a shame to be barren on the single day the Creator stands before you in need of food. It gives new meaning to being ready in season and out of season (2 Timothy 4:2). Jesus moves on without His hunger satisfied. His destination is the temple where He has a full day's work planned.

Just yesterday, Jesus surveyed the temple and the activity taking place there. But this is going to be the day He takes action to remedy the disgraceful denigration evidenced on the temple grounds. There is no indication that the disciples are helping Him, so we have a picture of the Savior singlehandedly and thoroughly sweeping through the whole place. He is decisive and unapologetic as He drives out the "robbers" in this house of prayer.

In this now clean environment, Jesus receives those in need of healing and relieves them of their afflictions. He is also teaching the crowds who have gathered, as Luke tells us He is doing each day (Luke 21:37). Those present aren't merely interested in what Jesus is saying; they are astonished by His words and manner. They can't put the pieces together that would reveal they are standing in the presence of God the Son. They can't grasp the import of His words or comprehend the implications of them. Still, they understand they have never in their lives heard anyone like Jesus.

Jesus retires for the night with His Father's House clean. The robbers will undoubtedly waste no time reestablishing themselves there, but today they are out on their ear. The dignity of the House of God is restored if even just for a day. Healed people lay their heads on their pillows free from what only this morning ailed them. The masses go to sleep with the words of Jesus still swirling in their minds. And the religious leaders end their day full of fury and fear. For now, they hunker down, plotting and waiting to strike.

Response:

Lord Jesus,

You led so powerfully on this day in history. You even commanded the attention of a tree, speaking to it so Your disciples could hear. Thank You for a look into Your heart that was determined to honor Your Father's House. Thank You for another glimpse into Your healing power. Thank You for the wisdom and truth that poured forth every time You opened Your mouth to speak. Thank You for, once again, showing me what it looks like to be outwardly focused, willing to work tirelessly on behalf of the Father. All praise to You, glorious Lord! ~ *Amen*

Remember:

_____

_____

_____

_____

_____

_____

_____

_____

_____

_____

Sunday
Day of Rest

WOES & LAMENTATION

Meditation:

Then Jesus said to the crowds and to His disciples,
"The scribes and the Pharisees sit on Moses'
seat, so do and observe whatever they
tell you, but not the works they do.
For they preach, but do not practice.
They tie up heavy burdens, hard to bear,
and lay them on people's shoulders,
but they themselves are not willing
to move them with their finger.
They do all their deeds to be seen by others.
O Jerusalem, Jerusalem, the city that kills the
prophets and stones those who are sent to it!"

~ MATTHEW 23:1–5

"But woe to you, scribes and Pharisees, hypocrites!
For you shut the kingdom of heaven in people's faces.
For you neither enter yourselves nor allow
those who would enter to go in. Woe to you,
scribes and Pharisees, hypocrites! For you travel
across sea and land to make a single proselyte,
and when he becomes a proselyte, you make
him twice as much a child of hell as yourselves."

~ MATTHEW 23:13–15

"How often would I have gathered your
children together as a hen gathers her brood
under her wings, and you were not willing!

See, your house is left to you desolate.
For I tell you, you will not see Me again, until you say,
'Blessed is He who comes in the name of the Lord.'"

~ MATTHEW 23:37-39

Reflection:

Jesus has just been telling stories in response to the petty accusations of His accusers. The parables recorded in three of the Gospels are pure gold to anyone able to decipher them. The stories expose hypocrisy, cruelty, corruption, and profound lack of stewardship. They also tell of the revolutionary ways of the Kingdom of God. Eventually the religious leaders clue into the fact that Jesus is exposing them, and they come unglued. But then Jesus begins to launch a direct attack in their direction.

The seven woes found in chapter 23 of Matthew are a blistering exposé of abuse and the price the abusers will pay. The abusers are the Scribes and Pharisees, the ones entrusted with the teaching and nurturing of the people of God. There is nothing left to the imagination as Jesus gives language to the depth of His disgust. Over and over, He repeats this phrase, "Woe to you, scribes and Pharisees, hypocrites!" and then He describes another thread of their corruption. A tender heart would be decimated by this exposure. Not so with the religious leaders. They are beside themselves with rage.

After having dispensed His words of woe, Jesus shows us once again the unquenchable love in His heart. He is heartbroken at the condition of His house and the people who live in it. Jesus is devastated, and so He laments. His words reveal what could have been had they been willing to open their hearts to Him. But it is now too late. The opportunity to experience and embrace God in the flesh has been squandered. The house of God and its willful occupants are desolate, laid waste and barren.

Three years of tireless pleading with the masses and the people of God end with Jesus lamenting. Is Jesus pleading with you to embrace Him? Is He exposing willfulness and hypocrisy in you? Is He asking you to surrender your will to His so that you can begin to truly live? Do not harden your heart. Let the words of Jesus about you be words of celebration and not lament. There is life and purpose to be found in Him and nowhere else. "I am the way, the truth and the life. No one comes to the Father except through Me" (John 14:6).

Response:

Lord Jesus,

I feel the intensity and danger in the words You spoke to those who claimed to follow God. I also feel the depth of love from Your heart as You lamented that day for all to hear. There is no one else who would pursue them or me like You do. No one else would care enough to expose the danger they created or that I create. And no one but You would lovingly invite a person out of danger into safety that only You can provide. I'm so sorry You endured such disregard when You were right there in person for people to touch and hear and talk to. I fear I, too, would have been among those who dismissed You. Today, I ask You for ears to hear Your voice and a heart eager to respond to You. I love You, Lord. *~Amen*

Remember:

_____

_____

_____

_____

_____

_____

_____

_____

A Look into the Future

Meditation:

And as He came out of the temple,
one of His disciples said to Him,
"Look, Teacher, what wonderful stones
and what wonderful buildings!"
And Jesus said to him, "Do you see these great
buildings? There will not be left here one stone
upon another that will not be thrown down."

~

And Jesus began to say to them,
"See that no one leads you astray.
Many will come in my name, saying,
'I am he!' and they will lead many astray."

~

"But be on your guard. For they will
deliver you over to councils, and
you will be beaten in synagogues, and
you will stand before governors and kings
for My sake, to bear witness before them.
For false christs and false prophets will arise
and perform signs and wonders, to
lead astray, if possible, the elect.
But be on guard; I have told you
all things beforehand."

~

"But concerning that day or that hour,
no one knows, not even the angels in heaven,
nor the Son, but only the Father.

Therefore stay awake—for you do not know
when the master of the house will come,
in the evening, or at midnight, or when the
rooster crows, or in the morning—
lest he come suddenly and find you asleep.
And what I say to you I say to all: Stay awake."

~ MARK 13:12; 5—6; 9; 22-23; 32; 35-37

Reflection:

Jesus has left the temple for the last time. His work there is finished, although most likely no one knows it but Him. He has said all there is to say. There is no need for more information, or signs and wonders, or truth for the crowds and religious leaders to consider. They've heard and seen enough from God Incarnate. It's been another long, emotional day. It's time to head out for the night as Jesus and the disciples have been doing for several days now.

Before they get out of the city, a disciple is waxing eloquent about the beauty of the temple. Jesus could have simply agreed with him. Instead, He launches into a prophetic dissertation that's going to leave them with images of destruction, torture, deception, falling away, and more. The crowds are gone; this is prophecy for His inner circle so that they will not be caught off guard when these things begin to take place. This is far above their heads at this point. The Holy Spirit will hold all these words to redeposit to them when they are ready to absorb them.

In two days, Jesus will be sharing Passover with these people. His tone will be different then. He will be nurturing;

but tonight He needs them to hear about the terrible things that will take place in their lifetime and beyond. They aren't putting all the pieces together in these moments. It isn't on their minds that when these terrible things happen Jesus will be absent from them. For now, Jesus needs them to start thinking about being ready, on their guard, and watchful. He needs them to start processing what it will mean to "stay awake." This prophetic news is apocalyptic. It is plenty heavy without the added burden of Jesus' impending departure from them. In this, we see Jesus taking very good care of His disciples.

Response:

Lord Jesus,

Your words to Your disciples were always the right words at the right time. It could be no other way. So it is with You and me. What do You want me to know as I consider these prophetic words? Many of them are yet to be fulfilled, and so I know that I too am to be watchful, on the lookout for the false teachers and false christs that will come. I too am to be watchful and ready for Your return. Please, Lord, help me by Your Holy Spirit to steward each day so that were You to come back, I would be found ready for You! ~*Amen*

Remember:

_____

_____

_____

_____

_____

_____

_____

_____

_____

_____

ANOINTED FOR BURIAL

Meditation:

Six days before the Passover, Jesus therefore came to Bethany,
where Lazarus was, whom Jesus had raised from the dead.
So they gave a dinner for Him there. Martha served,
and Lazarus was one of those reclining with Him at table.
Mary therefore took a pound of expensive ointment
made from pure nard, and anointed the feet of
Jesus and wiped His feet with her hair. The house
was filled with the fragrance of the perfume.
But Judas Iscariot, one of His disciples (he who was
about to betray Him), said, "Why was this ointment not
sold for three hundred denarii and given to the poor?"
He said this, not because he cared about the poor,
but because he was a thief, and having charge of the
moneybag he used to help himself to what was put into it.
Jesus said, "Leave her alone, so that she may keep it for the
day of My burial. For the poor you always have with you,
but you do not always have Me."

~ JOHN 12:1–8

Now when Jesus was at Bethany in the house of
Simon the leper, a woman came up to Him with an
alabaster flask of very expensive ointment, and she
poured it on His head as He reclined at table.
And when the disciples saw it, they were indignant,
saying, "Why this waste? For this could have been
sold for a large sum and given to the poor."
But Jesus, aware of this, said to them,

"Why do you trouble the woman?
For she has done a beautiful thing to Me.
For you always have the poor with you, but you will not
always have Me. In pouring this ointment on My body,
she has done it to prepare Me for burial. Truly, I say to you,
wherever this gospel is proclaimed in the whole world,
what she has done will also be told in memory of her."

~ MATTHEW 26:6-13

Reflection:

Jesus, full of resurrection power, makes reference in both these scenes to His own burial, and, therefore, to His impending death. This is a juxtaposition worth letting simmer for a while. It gives us a peek into the God/Man heading to Calvary. This tension is one we must be willing to carry throughout our journey to Easter. We must choose not to forget that God the Son is submitting to the will of God the Father, allowing things to happen to Him that He is fully capable of overturning. We must purpose to follow the events about to unfold, remembering that Jesus is God the Son, come in human form.

There is so much going on in these two scenes. One is a "Thank You, Jesus" meal hosted by three siblings, Mary, Martha and Lazarus, friends of Jesus. He is obviously the guest of honor. Lazarus (formerly dead!), casually reclines at the table. Martha is serving, but not complaining about it as she once would have. Mary is still at Jesus' side, displaying her extravagant love again, this time anointing Him with very expensive perfume. Four days later, Jesus is the guest of honor for a meal at Simon the leper's house. Here a woman comes and pours a very costly oil of pure nard (the same oil that Mary used) on Jesus' head.

Those in attendance on both occasions make up a vastly diverse group. Friends, foes, enlightened and ignorant, all are present with varying agendas. The disciple Judas, who the passage in John tells us is a thief and the betrayer, is his typical masterfully deceptive self, calling out Mary's actions as grossly wasteful. The other disciples come to the same conclusion at Simon's house after the woman pours the nard on the head of Jesus. It begs the question, how on earth do they miss the glaring similarity in these two scenes, setting themselves up for the same rebuke Jesus gave Judas four nights earlier?

Neither Judas' hypocrisy nor the other disciples' ignorance bear any weight. Jesus seizes both awkward moments, telling the opposers to back off and why. Just about everyone misses the meaning and the import of Jesus' words. He is telling them the future, but most of them are occupied in the minutia of the moment.

These were far more than meals with friends. And they were significant far beyond the comprehension of the attendees. These private gatherings became ceremonies in which the Son of Man's body would be prepared for death and burial. Imagine the scene if those in attendance had understood. Imagine the awe and wonder and reverence that would have been rightly paid to their Lord.

Response:

Lord Jesus,

I'm certain I miss most of the treasure You lay before me, just as those in these stories did. I don't want to do that as I meditate with You in the remembrance of these two gatherings. Please show me something of the sacredness of these two preparatory anointings. Show me something of Your beauty in them. Show me more about these two women, infinitely more clued in than anyone else, save You. I want to learn. I want to learn so that I don't miss the moments You put before me. And I want to learn because I want to know You more and worship You with more of my heart. Please speak to me. ~ *Amen*

Remember:

_____

_____

_____

_____

_____

_____

_____

Glorifying the Father

Meditation:

"Now is My soul troubled. And what shall I say? 'Father, save Me from this hour?' But for this purpose I have come to this hour. Father, glorify Your name." Then a voice came from heaven: "I have glorified it, and I will glorify it again."

~

And Jesus cried out and said, "Whoever believes in Me, believes not in Me but in Him who sent Me. And whoever sees Me sees Him who sent Me. I have come into the world as light, so that whoever believes in Me may not remain in darkness. If anyone hears My words and does not keep them, I do not judge him; for I did not come to judge the world but to save the world. The one who rejects Me and does not receive My words has a judge; the word that I have spoken will judge him on the last day. For I have not spoken on My own authority, but the Father who sent Me has Himself given Me a commandment —what to say and what to speak. And I know that His commandment is eternal life. What I say, therefore, I say as the Father has told Me."

~ JOHN 12:27-28; 44-50

Reflection:

What would be foremost in your mind if you knew that the following evening you would be arrested and put to death? What if you had one more shot at speaking to the masses of humanity? How would you spend your last opportunity to influence people? The passages above describe that very day in Jesus' life. That same evening Jesus will go to His friend Simon's house for dinner. By then, His public ministry will be complete. Tomorrow is Passover. In two days, Jesus will be buried in a tomb.

I am deeply struck that time and again in this last public forum, Jesus reveals His occupation with thoughts of His Father. Jesus' soul is troubled, knowing what He is moving toward. He could ask the Father to spare Him from having to endure the impending sequence of events. Instead, there is an almost nostalgic tone to Jesus' words: *Father, glorify Your name.* Jesus is about to enter the torturous events that will take Him to Calvary, and His utmost desire is that His Father will glorify Himself! Selah!

Then Jesus turns His words to the people there to see Him. The passage says that He cries out to them. What kind of urgency must He be feeling as He looks upon this gathering? This is it! This is the last verbal plea. He tells them He came to bring light, that He came not to judge but to save. He wants them to understand that belief in Him is synonymous with belief in the Father. He goes out of His way to link Himself with the Father as He did so many times before. He is longing for them to make this connection.

Finally, Jesus emphatically states (and not for the first time) that every action He takes and every word He speaks is done at the behest of the Father. It's another vantage point to emphasize the reality of the eternal bond Father and Son maintain. To be given even this faint glimpse of these two persons of the Trinity is a gift beyond measure. The Father champions the Son. The Son is ever seeking to make much of the Father.

Response:

Lord Jesus,

This passage of Your story is so filled with wonder. Speak to me about the bond between You and the Father. It's a bond innate between each of the persons of the Trinity, but so foreign to selfish humans. You were intent that the Father glorify Himself through You, and He did! And He was intent that you be lifted up so that every knee would bow at Your feet. I give You praise, Jesus! I honor You and the Father and the Holy Spirit. Please glorify Yourself through me. Guide me, Holy Spirit, to that end! ~*Amen*

Remember:

Jesus, Love to the End

Meditation:

Now before the Feast of the Passover, when Jesus
knew that His hour had come to depart out of this
world to the Father, having loved His own who
were in the world, He loved them to the end.
During supper, when the devil had already put it into
the heart of Judas Iscariot, Simon's son, to betray Him,
Jesus, knowing that the Father had given all things
into His hands, and that He had come from God
and was going back to God, rose from supper.
He laid aside His outer garments, and taking a towel,
tied it around His waist. Then He poured water into a
basin and began to wash the disciples' feet and to wipe
them with the towel that was wrapped around Him.
When He had washed their feet and put on His outer
garments and resumed His place, He said to them,
"Do you understand what I have done to you?
You call me Teacher and Lord, and you are right,
for so I am. If I then, your Lord and Teacher,
have washed your feet, you also ought to wash
one another's feet. For I have given you an example,
that you also should do just as I have done to you.
Truly, truly, I say to you, a servant is not greater
than his master, nor is a messenger greater than the
one who sent him. If you know these things,
blessed are you if you do them.

~ JOHN 13:1–5; 12–17

Reflection:

With Jesus' public ministry behind Him, He turns now to His inner circle as they gather to share Passover together. The disciples have no clue what these hours are going to bring. But Jesus, taking His cues from the Father, has a detailed agenda. The apostle John puts the whole thing in context with these two insights into Jesus' thinking. First, Jesus knows He is about to depart this world. Secondly, He is about to show His followers what it looks like to love someone "to the end" (John 13:1).

Pause for several minutes to let these two insights settle into your mind. All that is going to happen in the upper room and in the garden launches from Jesus' impending departure and the depth of His love for His followers. That means no matter where you stop in the story, your observations will be greatly enhanced. You will find the deeply relational heart of God the Son on display, consumed with the desires of the Father and the care of His people.

And so it begins. God in human form, with all power and authority in His grasp, performs a menial service for men He has been leading for three years. He is their Master. They call Him Lord. He is doing what no master would ever do for a servant. He uses His own garment and, one by one, washes twelve sets of dirty feet. It is an act of service, hospitality, and respect. Through it, He is teaching them (and us) something revolutionary.

The foot washing isn't an object lesson, although is suffices very well as one. It is an act of genuine love—love that no human could possibly perform or even desire to express apart from God in them. Genuine love can only derive from its Source. It upturns human value systems. It proves that our unthinkable is God's normal. It is entirely selfless, which is very unsettling for thoroughly selfish people. It is, in a word, *revolutionary*. Jesus has been talking about it and demonstrating it time and again in His public and private life. Tonight, the utter otherness of the love of God has a brand new layer.

Response:

Lord Jesus,

What You did for the disciples that night came from a place inside You that I don't know if I will ever understand. But I'd like to know more than I do now. I feel if I could understand even a little more, I might grow in my appreciation of You. Will You tell me more about that first act of love in the upper room? You've told me that I should do just what You have done. You've told me to love like You love. Help me to do that. I worship You, Jesus. The purity and otherness of Your love has been lost on me for too long. Bring light to my eyes, I pray. ~*Amen*

Remember:

_____

_____

_____

_____

_____

Jesus the Friend

Meditation:

"This is my commandment, that you love one
nother as I have loved you. Greater love has no one
than this, that someone lay down his life for his friends.
You are My friends if you do what I command you.
No longer do I call you servants, for the servant does
not know what his master is doing; but I have called
you friends, for all that I have heard from my Father
I have made known to you. You did not choose me,
but I chose you and appointed you that you should
go and bear fruit and that your fruit should abide,
so that whatever you ask the Father in my name,
He may give it to you. These things I command
you, so that you will love one another."

~ JOHN 15:12–17

"I have manifested Your name to the people whom
You gave me out of the world. Yours they were, and You
gave them to Me, and they have kept Your word. Now they
know that everything that You have given Me is from You.
For I have given them the words that You gave Me,
and they have received them and have come to know in
truth that I came from You; and they have believed
that You sent me. I am praying for them."

~ JOHN 17:6–9

Reflection:

When Jesus dies at Calvary, His companions lose not only their Master and Teacher, but their Friend. What would it be like to be befriended by the sinless Savior and experience His friendship? A prayerful read through the gospels looking for Jesus, the friend, would yield more than we might imagine.

Only a few hours before the Lord will be betrayed and arrested, He speaks to His disciples about friendship. It is important enough to Him to be included in these final exchanges (John 15). It will also be very much on His mind as He speaks to the Father in what we refer to as his high priestly prayer (John 17). The care He takes of His followers both in person and in prayer is astonishing in light of what He is about to endure. But apparently that is one of the qualities of true friendship, giving no thought to oneself when one's friends are in need.

Have we thanked Jesus lately for His friendship to us? We can survive in life without friendship, but we cannot appreciate the gift it is to be alive—without it. How very loving of God to include friendship as one of the ways He relates with us.

Jesus does not have to approach us as friends, but it pleases Him to do so. It's one of the ways He tells us He loves us. And, of course, His friendship is like no other, with qualities we will never experience with anyone else in the same way we will with Him. It is worthy to contemplate the friendship of the Son of God as Easter approaches.

Response:

Lord Jesus,

You are the friend who sticks closer than a brother (Proverbs 18:24). You are the friend who laid down His life as a demonstration of His love (John 15:12). You are the One who prays for His friends (John 17:9). That You would approach me with a gift of friendship is inconceivable to me. How can I possibly thank You? Teach me about the beauty of this gift and help me steward it to bring You glory. ~Amen

Remember:

Sunday
Day of Rest

JESUS THE TEACHER

Meditation:

"For I have not spoken on My own authority,
but the Father who sent Me has himself given me a
commandment —what to say and what to speak.
And I know that His commandment is eternal life.
What I say, therefore, I say as the Father has told Me."

~ JOHN 12:49-50

"I am the vine; you are the branches. Whoever abides
in Me and I in him, he it is that bears much fruit, for apart
from Me you can do nothing. If anyone does not abide in
Me he is thrown away like a branch and withers; and the
branches are gathered, thrown into the fire, and burned.
If you abide in Me, and My words abide in you,
ask whatever you wish, and it will be done for you.
By this my Father is glorified, that you bear much fruit
and so prove to be My disciples. As the Father has loved Me,
so have I loved you. Abide in My love. If you keep My
commandments, you will abide in My love, just as I have
kept My Father's commandments and abide in His love.
These things I have spoken to you, that My joy may
be in you, and that your joy may be full."

~ JOHN 15:5-11

Reflection:

As we saturate ourselves in the life of Jesus in the days leading up to His arrest and death, let's consider how He tends

to His followers as their teacher. All those who listen to Jesus teach throughout His three years of public life have the gift of hearing the greatest Teacher who will ever live. But few have the added gift of watching Him live His life behind the scenes. Those who do, witness the flawless execution of everything Jesus teaches in public. He lives what He preaches.

For all the diversity of Jesus's teaching in these final days, a few thoughts have surfaced for me that have launched from the scripture passages above. The first is this: most teachers work from a curriculum that is not their own. Jesus makes it very clear He is no different. While He is in complete agreement with all He speaks, the instruction He gives comes exclusively from the Father, and He makes sure everyone understands that. Whatever is important to the Father is important to Jesus. Jesus has a specific agenda, but it is not His own. It is NEVER His own (note to self).

In case His followers (that means us, too) can't make the connection between how He lives and how *they* are supposed to live, Jesus teaches them using a very comprehensive analogy. John chapter 15 might be one of the most familiar passages of scripture there is. A vinedresser, a vine, a branch connected to that vine, and the nutrients that flow though the vine: it's a picture of connectivity that drives home our comprehensive need of God.

Jesus' life of deference and submission to the Father is not a path among other paths for fruitful living. It is the singular path to fulfilling His life purpose. The same holds true for us. Our own deference and submission will ensure that we will live the way we are designed to live, bearing fruit by abiding in Christ.

Jesus' teaching days are far from over. You and I are meant to glean from Him no less powerfully than those who literally walked the earth with Him. My hope is that as we prayerfully sit with the passages above, we will experience Jesus as the attentive, perfect teacher He is.

Response:

Lord Jesus,

Will You teach me as You did those who walked the earth with You? I understand, however faintly, that if I'm going to live out the things You teach me, it's going to happen as I abide in You. Teach me more about what it means to abide. Teach me more about how You practiced that kind of abiding. Thank You that You continued to be such an attentive Teacher to your followers, even as You approached the cross. And now, as I approach the remembrance of Your death, I praise You for being the great teacher You are! *~Amen*

Remember:

_____

_____

_____

_____

_____

_____

_____

JESUS THE CAREGIVER

Meditation:

"My children, I will be with you only a little
longer. You will look for Me, and just as I told
the Jews, so I tell you now: Where I am going,
you cannot come. Where I am going, you cannot
follow now, but you will follow later."

~ JOHN 13:33; 36

"I will not leave you as orphans; I will come to you.
Before long, the world will not see Me anymore,
but you will see Me. Because I live, you also will live."

~ JOHN 14:18–19

"I have told you this so that My joy may be
in you and that your joy may be complete."

~ JOHN 15:11

"All this I have told you so that you will not
fall away. I have told you these things,
so that in Me you may have peace.
In this world you will have trouble.
But take heart! I have overcome the world."

~ JOHN 16:1; 33

"Holy Father, protect them by the power
of Your name, the name You gave Me,
so that they may be one as We are one.
While I was with them, I protected them
and kept them safe by that name You gave Me."

~ JOHN 17:11–12

Reflection:

No one cares for people like Jesus does. His care is comprehensive, so that while He is with His followers, they have need of nothing. But especially in the hours He shares with the disciples in the upper room and in the garden, Jesus provides a quality of care that ought to leave us in awe. Jesus is meeting needs His disciples don't even know they have yet. There is no way they can understand His provision. Jesus never wavers in His generosity and tender care even though He knows He will be betrayed and profoundly neglected by those He's providing for. With His death approaching, Jesus remains as focused as ever, nurturing those the Father has entrusted to Him.

I'm encouraging all of us to spend time meditating upon John chapters thirteen through seventeen, asking the Lord to speak to us about Himself as caregiver. The whole objective of caregiving is to do for one what they are incapable of doing for themselves, either because they don't know they are in need or because they are unable to do for themselves. That warrants a pause.

I wonder if we have an adequate awareness of our need of God so that we understand He isn't just being nice to us, but providing what no one else could possibly provide. I know I can fight Him, just like a child does when they are feeling especially independent. But I always cheat myself when I do. Maybe you can relate. No doubt there is room in all of us for growth in our level of gratitude for His flawless, all-encompassing care. No one cares like Jesus. Absolutely no one.

Response:

Lord Jesus,

    You are the ultimate caregiver. Open my eyes as I read the account of all that took place in the upper room. I wait upon You. Please speak to me today about the beauty of the care You took of Your followers in those precious hours you spent together. And Lord, You care for me like no one could possibly care for me. I praise You and thank You for Your lavish care. I need what You provide. But, Lord, You give over and above the need. Thank You. I know I take Your care of me for granted. Please help me to gain ground here so that my gratitude grows. As my gratitude increases, help me to worship You more as You deserve to be worshiped. *~Amen*

Remember:

_____

_____

_____

_____

_____

_____

Jesus, the Comforter

Meditation:

"Do not let your hearts be troubled.
You believe in God; believe also in Me.
My Father's house has many rooms; if that
were not so, would I have told you that I am
going there to prepare a place for you?
And if I go and prepare a place for you,
I will come back and take you to be with
Me that you also may be where I am.
You know the way to the place where I am going.
I am the way and the truth and the life.
No one comes to the Father except through Me.
Peace I leave with you; My peace I give you.
I do not give to you as the world gives. Do not
let your hearts be troubled and do not be afraid."

~ JOHN 14:1-4; 6: 27

"None of you asks me, 'Where are You going?'
Rather, you are filled with grief because I have said these
things. But very truly I tell you, it is for your good that I am
going away. Unless I go away, the Advocate will not come to
you; but if I go, I will send Him to you. I have much more
to say to you, more than you can now bear. But when He,
the Spirit of truth, comes, He will guide you into all the
truth. He will not speak on His own; He will speak only
what He hears, and He will tell you what is yet to come.
He will glorify Me because it is from Me that He will receive
what He will make known to you. Very truly I tell you,

you will weep and mourn while the world rejoices.
You will grieve, but your grief will turn to joy.
A woman giving birth to a child has pain because
her time has come; but when her baby is
born she forgets the anguish because of her
joy that a child is born into the world.
So with you: Now is your time of grief,
but I will see you again and you will rejoice,
and no one will take away your joy."

~ JOHN 16:5-7; 12-14; 20-22

Reflection:

From the moment Jesus and His disciples sit down to have their last meal together, Jesus starts engaging with His disciples: instructing, encouraging, informing, rallying, comforting. He is giving them the download of all downloads knowing full well the necessity of His words. But much of Jesus' words are difficult and unsettling. As their dialogue progresses, a sense of grief begins to set in. No one but Jesus understands the breadth of the fears taking hold and the sense of panic growing within His inner circle. And Jesus is prepared to do all He can to assuage their angst by comforting them.

Imagine having *only* the right words, *only* the right body language, *only* the right countenance, *only* the right tone of voice. Jesus has everything His friends need as they begin to grieve. The idea that they would be separated from Him is devastating. They certainly have no idea how much worse things are going to get in the next twenty-four hours. But

Jesus knows, and He is speaking into their lives in a way that brings comfort both in the moment and again after He will die.

I've been thinking about the fact that part of their conversation is about the coming of the Holy Spirit, who Jesus calls the Comforter or Advocate. The Father will send them the Spirit, even as the Father sent Jesus to them. Jesus says that the Spirit will "glorify Me because it is from Me that He will receive what He will make known to you" (John 16:14). Jesus has no intention of leaving His followers without the comfort they have come to rely upon. In some unexplainable way, the coming of the Comforter will actually be an upgrade (John 16:7), though that will be impossible for them to imagine in the moment. Equally unimaginable is the fact that the comfort of the Holy Spirit will come to them as the express representative of Jesus, as powerfully as if Jesus were to remain among them.

Response:

Lord Jesus,

Thank You for the beauty of Your comfort. Thank You for the gift that Your comfort was to Your disciples and is to me! You never leave us in our grief. You are by our side, comforting us in a way that only You can. Speak to me today about the beauty of Your comforting nature as You spent those many hours preparing Your disciples for Your departure. I worship You, God of all comfort! ~Amen

Remember:

_____

_____

_____

_____

_____

_____

_____

Sorrowful Even to Death

Meditation:

Then Jesus went with them to a place called
Gethsemane, and He said to his disciples,
"Sit here, while I go over there and pray."
And taking with Him Peter and the two sons of
Zebedee, He began to be sorrowful and troubled.
Then He said to them, "My soul is very sorrowful,
even to death; remain here, and watch with Me."
And going a little farther He fell on His face and prayed,
saying, "My Father, if it be possible, let this cup pass
from Me; nevertheless, not as I will, but as You will."
And He came to the disciples and found them sleeping.
And He said to Peter, "So, could you not watch with
Me one hour? Watch and pray that you may not enter into
temptation. The spirit indeed is willing, but the flesh is
weak." Again, for the second time, He went away and
prayed, "My Father, if this cannot pass unless I drink it,
Your will be done." And again He came and found
them sleeping, for their eyes were heavy.
So, leaving them again, He went away and prayed
for the third time, saying the same words again.
Then He came to the disciples and said to them,
"Sleep and take your rest later on. See, the hour is
at hand, and the Son of Man is betrayed into the
hands of sinners. Rise, let us be going;
see, My betrayer is at hand."

~ MATTHEW 26:36–46

(SEE ALSO MARK 14:32–41; LUKE 22:39–46)

Reflection:

The garden of Gethsemane is ground Zero for a few of the most critical hours in all of history. After the comprehensive instructions and care given by Jesus to His disciples, Jesus draws away to pray, becoming profoundly distressed. Judas Iscariot is carrying out his betrayal, and Jesus' arrest is impending.

Jesus' confession of the depth of His suffering to His closest friends is striking. I wonder how they deal with His extreme vulnerability with them. There isn't one recorded word that tells us they are able to provide consolation. They are in their own distress, likely trying to process the words Jesus spoke to them. The gospel of Luke tells us they actually fall asleep "from sorrow" (Luke 22:45). The hours pass with Jesus moving between the location of His friends and His place of prayer, all the while He's experiencing the escalation of His own sorrow.

I marvel that while Jesus is enduring this level of anguish, He is still managing to be Friend, Teacher, Caregiver, and Comforter to His inner circle. He prevails in His own battle where His friends fail in theirs, even with Jesus' frequent cautioning. I sympathize with the disciples in the garden, glad it was not me asked to watch and pray. I would have failed Him, too.

For me, these few hours in the garden are among the most heart-wrenching in all of scripture. The physiological suffering Jesus bears would be the death of anyone else. Can you fathom enduring anguish even to death and remaining submitted to the will of God? Can you imagine pleading with the Father for another way to fulfill your mission, under that level of duress, but not losing your resolve to honor God? There will never be anyone like Jesus! Not ever!

Response:

Lord Jesus,

Praise You, my suffering Savior. It is beyond me to understand the depths of what You endured in Gethsemane. As I picture You in prayer that evening, I'm blown away that there is space for Your honest pleas to the Father, but there is not space within You to move against His will. There is truly no one like You. And now, Lord, speak to me. What do You want me to know about those hours in Gethsemane? Teach me as I meditate on Your Word. ~*Amen*

Remember:

_____

_____

_____

_____

_____

_____

_____

The War in Gethsemane
The Battle of the Flesh

Meditation:

> And when the devil had ended every temptation,
> he departed from Him until an opportune time.
>
> ~ LUKE 4:13

> And when He came to the place, He said to them,
> "Pray that you may not enter into temptation."
> And He withdrew from them about a stone's
> throw, and knelt down and prayed, saying,
> "Father, if You are willing, remove this cup from Me.
> Nevertheless, not My will, but Yours, be done."
> And there appeared to Him an angel from heaven,
> strengthening Him. And being in agony He
> prayed more earnestly; and His sweat became like
> great drops of blood falling down to the ground.
>
> ~ LUKE 22:40-44

> "Watch and pray that you may not enter into temptation.
> The spirit indeed is willing, but the flesh is weak."
>
> ~ MARK 14:38

Reflection:

We will look at these same texts for two days from two different vantage points. First, we see Jesus the man, under duress like no one has ever experienced. Then, tomorrow, we will focus on one of the final battles waged over evil itself. Take another few minutes and re-read the above passages with a picture of Jesus, the human being, in your mind. What would a human be experiencing under these circumstances? Let the Holy Spirit drop you into this scene.

We must remind ourselves that Jesus sets aside His deity and takes the form of a man. He relinquishes the exercising of His power and relies upon the power of God the Spirit. He relinquishes the exercising of His will and follows the lead of God the Father. He is the God/Man acting as a man. And this Man is facing what no man has ever had to face. The sheer emotional wight of His impending horror takes Jesus to the brink of death. It's one thing to face death. It's another altogether to experience duress so extreme, you could die from it.

So Jesus asks that the cup might be removed. Not once, not twice, but three times. The anguish itself is killing Him. He looks for solace from His human friends. He does that more than once. But there is none to be found. Instead, He finds three men in need of *Him*, unable to aid Him in His hour of need. There is nothing on the earth, no created being or thing that is able to bring comfort to our Lord. He is alone and utterly bereft of help. And yet...

The Holy Spirit does for Jesus what Jesus chooses not to do for Himself. He shores Him up in His inner man. He ministers to Him in His psychological distress. He sustains Him physically and comforts Him. He does for Jesus what is necessary so that the weakened flesh will not utterly fail. The battle is won. Jesus will leave the garden victorious.

Response:

Lord Jesus,

As I see the garden in my mind, my eyes are drawn to You. You are suffering beyond understanding. You are abandoned by Your friends. You are alone in the human realm. I know nothing of the anguish You endure or the sorrow of Your soul. But I praise You, victorious One! You prevail in those most torturous hours by the power of God the Spirit. Praise You! Thank You for showing me what's possible by the power of the Holy Spirit! *~Amen*

Remember:

_____

_____

_____

_____

_____

_____

_____

_____

_____

_____

THE WAR IN GETHSEMANE
THE BATTLE OF THE AGES

Meditation:

And when the devil had ended every temptation,
he departed from Him until an opportune time.

~ LUKE 4:13

And when He came to the place, He said to them,
"Pray that you may not enter into temptation."
And He withdrew from them about a stone's
throw, and knelt down and prayed, saying,
"Father, if You are willing, remove this cup from Me.
Nevertheless, not My will, but Yours, be done."
And there appeared to Him an angel from
heaven, strengthening Him. And being in agony
He prayed more earnestly; and His sweat became like
great drops of blood falling down to the ground.

~ LUKE 22:40–44

Watch and pray that you may not enter into temptation.
The spirit indeed is willing, but the flesh is weak.

~ MARK 14:38

Reflection:

Jesus' humanity is stretched to the tearing point as He
repeatedly asks, *"Let this cup pass from Me."* If these hours
are the "opportune time" referenced in Luke chapter 4, then
the attack that Satan wages in the garden is unprecedented.

This will end up being the last opportunity for the adversary to dissuade Jesus from going to the cross, and Jesus will never be more vulnerable than He is here in the garden.

Even so, Jesus does not come to Gethsemane unprepared. He is battle ready. He is strong in the Spirit and His ears are tuned to the voice of His Father. He is practiced in battle. The Word of God is in His heart, ready to come to bear as He fights. He knows the ways of His enemy and so He does not deal with shock or disorientation when encountering Satan. That does not diminish the brutality of this engagement, but it means that Jesus is in the fight on the offensive from its inception, not having to spend any time orienting to an attack.

Jesus begins to speak to His Father in prayer. This is the first most potent line of offense in the battle. He invites Peter, James, and John to be within earshot of His prayers, allowing them to practice resisting the tempting presence permeating that garden space. Their souls too are sorrowful. Jesus knows that and instructs them to do what He is going to be doing. Here, both Savior and those being saved are allowed to be tested by the great tempter, their weakened flesh being Satan's point of entry.

The collision of forces battling this evening in both the seen and unseen worlds represent the battle of the ages, literally. The whole course of history is about to dramatically shift, sealing the fate of the adversary once and for all, bringing the hope of real redemption to humanity.

Nothing that is taking place here in the garden is unknown to The Father. The strategy of battle has been in place from eternity, and God knows He will win. Jesus, by the power of the Holy Spirit and the help of a ministering angel, stays the course throughout the entire ordeal in Gethsemane. In these final moments before His arrest, while He still has time to opt out, Jesus stays the course!

Response:

Lord Jesus,

You were prepared for this battle. How many times do I come to a battle completely caught off guard? Not so with You! And You were not alone in the battle. You relied upon the Spirit and the loving guidance of the Father to provide what Your flesh could not provide. The evil one came at You with the best he had to offer and he utterly failed. Teach me, Lord. I want to be more like You. I give You all praise and glory! ~Amen

Remember:

_____

_____

_____

_____

_____

_____

Sunday
Day of Rest

THE ARREST OF JESUS

Meditation:

So Judas, having procured a band of soldiers and
some officers from the chief priests and the Pharisees,
went there with lanterns and torches and weapons.
Then Jesus, knowing all that would happen to Him,
came forward and said to them, "Whom do you seek?"
They answered him, "Jesus of Nazareth."
Jesus said to them, "I am He."
Judas, who betrayed Him, was standing with them.
When Jesus said to them, "I am He,"
they drew back and fell to the ground.
So He asked them again, "Whom do you seek?"
And they said, "Jesus of Nazareth."
Jesus answered, "I told you that I am He.
So, if you seek Me, let these men go."
This was to fulfill the word that He had spoken:
"Of those whom You gave Me I have lost not one."
Then Simon Peter, having a sword, drew it and struck
the high priest's servant and cut off his right ear.
(The servant's name was Malchus.) So Jesus said to
Peter, "Put your sword into its sheath; shall I not
drink the cup that the Father has given Me?"

~ JOHN 18:3-11

At that hour Jesus said to the crowds,
"Have you come out as against a robber,
with swords and clubs to capture Me?
Day after day I sat in the temple teaching,
and you did not seize Me.

But all this has taken place that the
Scriptures of the prophets might be fulfilled."
Then all the disciples left him and fled.

~ MATTHEW 26:55–56

Then Jesus said to the chief priests and
officers of the temple and elders,
who had come out against Him,
"Have you come out as against a robber,
with swords and clubs? When I was with
you day after day in the temple, you did
not lay hands on Me. But this is your hour,
and the power of darkness."

~ LUKE 22:52–53

(SEE ALSO: MATTHEW 26:47–56; MARK 14:42–50; LUKE 22:47–53)

Reflection:

All four of the gospels give us a look into the scene that takes place in the garden. Betrayal, confrontation, violence, healing, abandonment—all are part of the moments of Jesus' arrest. But Jesus is calm and poised and definitely in charge here in the company of His captors.

Jesus is ready to face His arrest head on. He has prepared Himself through prayer. He stands in the power of the Holy Spirit. He is strengthened through the tending of an angelic being. There will be no more asking for another way, and so as His accusers approach along with their substantial reinforcements, Jesus makes an offensive move toward them. In doing so, He disarms them immediately. He does this not through force, but through His authoritative presence. His declaration: "I am He," sends them backward and to the ground. Jesus is the master of the moment.

After Jesus secures the safety of the disciples, Peter draws his sword and cuts the ear off of a servant. Not a soldier, mind you, but the servant of the high priest. This is a useless, misguided step that ends up being Peter's final attempt at demonstrating his loyalty to Jesus. Jesus puts the ear back on the man and rebukes Peter. What a scene.

The contrast between the small army there to overpower Jesus if need be and the befuddled group of sleepy disciples reveals the gross incomprehension of those on both sides. No one seems to understand whose presence they are in. Not so for the celestial and demonic population. They are acutely aware that Jesus is God the Son.

This is the accuser's "hour, and the power of darkness." But his limited power is under the watchful eye and controlling hand of God! Every step Jesus takes toward the cross, beginning right here with His arrest, He takes as the One in the controlling position. The enemy cannot help but play into the hand of God.

Response:

Lord Jesus,

There in the garden, in the moments surrounding Your arrest, You were magnificent. Praise You, Jesus, who allowed Yourself to be led as a lamb to the slaughter (Isaiah 53:7). You were enacting the plan that You made with the Father from eternity. They were fools who thought they were getting the better of You that evening. Now speak to me, Lord! Here in Your presence, what would you have me see, or feel, or hear as I ponder the story of Your arrest? ~*Amen*

Remember:

_____

_____

_____

_____

_____

_____

_____

_____

_____

_____

THE SUPREME PERVERSION
OF JUSTICE

Meditation:

Then those who had seized Jesus led Him to Caiaphas the
high priest, where the scribes and the elders had gathered.
And Peter was following Him at a distance, as far as the
courtyard of the high priest, and going inside he sat with
the guards to see the end. Now the chief priests and the
whole council were seeking false testimony against Jesus
that they might put Him to death, but they found
none, though many false witnesses came forward.

~ MATTHEW 26:57-60

(SEE ALSO: MATTHEW 26:57 - 27:26; MARK 14:53 - 15:15;
LUKE 22:54 - 23:25; JOHN 18:12 - 19:16)

Reflection:

Very soon we will focus on the words of Jesus to the various
authority figures He stood before. In the meantime, let's get
reacquainted with the narrative found in the four passages
at the top of today's entry. I encourage you not to skip any
of them; otherwise, you will miss some critical pieces of
what's recorded for us.

There is so much activity surrounding the hours Jesus
is moved from place to place until He is finally sentenced
to death. Six trials take place over the course of eight or
nine hours. Three Jewish religious trials render three guilty
verdicts including a death sentence. Conversely, trials with

Pilate, then Herod, then Pilate again all find Jesus innocent of any wrongdoing.

A read through each of the gospel narratives will have anyone with a justice meter dumbfounded by the absence of anything resembling justice. There is not a single aspect of the content of these hours that is in alignment with the Jewish judicial system God established (Deuteronomy 16:18-20). It stands as the greatest perversion of justice in history.

The friends of Jesus are silent in Jesus' defense, if not absent altogether. Peter is looking from a safe distance that turns out not to be so safe. The rest of the disciples are off the grid. The Jewish leaders are clearly ready to do anything at all to see Jesus put to death. The Roman authorities are the least offensive, even though Pilate finally cowers to the riotous crowd and gives Jesus up to be executed. Jesus, and Jesus alone, is the single ray of light in the whole mad scene.

Response:

Lord Jesus,

As I open these passages in Your presence, I ask You to allow the narrative to seep into my heart. This is a huge, terrible sequence of events and perversion of justice. You endured so much and on so many levels, all the while pressing forward toward the cross. True colors were flying for everyone that day. Only You flew the colors of the Kingdom of God. My heart breaks. Forgive Your people, Lord. Forgive me. I'm so sorry that your closest friends, so riddled with fear, left Your side. And yet all of that sin was before Your eyes. It is the reason You came and did what You did. You were about to pay for these acts of betrayal and injustice. There is no one like You! And now I glorify You, Jesus, for the immeasurable sacrifice You made. You made it willingly and all for the joy set before You (Hebrews 12:2). Thank You, Jesus! ~*Amen*

Remember:

_____

_____

_____

_____

_____

_____

_____

_____

_____

_____

_____

He Opened Not His Mouth

Meditation:

> He was oppressed, and He was afflicted,
> yet He opened not His mouth; like a lamb that is
> led to the slaughter, and like a sheep that before its
> shearers is silent, so He opened not his mouth.
>
> ~ ISAIAH 53:7

> He will not cry aloud or lift up his voice,
> or make it heard in the street.
>
> ~ ISAIAH 42:2

> But when He was accused by the chief priests and elders,
> He gave no answer. Then Pilate said to Him, "Do You
> not hear how many things they testify against You?"
> But He gave him no answer, not even to a single charge,
> so that the governor was greatly amazed.
>
> ~ MATTHEW 27:12–14

> When Herod saw Jesus, he was very glad, for he had long
> desired to see Him, because he had heard about Him,
> and he was hoping to see some sign done by Him.
> So he questioned Him at some length, but He
> made no answer. The chief priests and the scribes
> stood by, vehemently accusing Him.
>
> ~ LUKE 23:8–10

> "What is it that these men testify against You?"
> But He remained silent and made no answer.
>
> ~ MARK 14:60–63

Reflection:

What happens instinctively to you when you are falsely accused? What if you know you are going to be killed for these falsehoods? Do your self-preservation instincts kick in? What does Jesus do as this happens to Him? Jesus' instincts default to the will of the Father. They are submitted to His will. Selah. So what *is* the Father's desire for Jesus in the face of a litany of trumped-up charges?

For every false accusation put to Jesus, not a word is spoken in reply. He does not refute or defend. He does not try to explain or correct. He remains silent. Annas, Pilate, Herod, and the swarm of Jewish leaders spewing their hate speech receive no satisfaction whatsoever from Jesus. Herod is hoping for a magic show and gets nothing at all. While the accusers' fury escalates, Jesus remains poised. And we cannot forget that all the while Jesus is being subjected to merciless taunting and physical abuse.

Once again, our justice meter spikes. Jesus is capable of refuting these ridiculous lies, but He doesn't, not even one time. The lack of response makes Him appear weak to the reader, but I don't know that He appeared that way at all in actuality. And perhaps that is what causes the religious leaders to escalate in their fury toward Him. They cannot seem to unsettle Him or cause Him to weaken. Silence is a powerful language of its own in this case, and Jesus remains strong in His resolve to hold His words, even as He weakens physically through the beatings. Jesus' determination to keep moving in the direction of Golgotha is ironclad. The garden is behind Him and the fulfillment of His mission is just ahead.

Response:

Lord Jesus,

Your actions in this part of the story are a mystery to me. I believe You are doing exactly what You mean to do, but still I wish You could set the record straight in these moments of injustice and false accusations. You are laser-focused. Nothing is going to detour You from moving along the path the Father has set before You. I'm in awe of You. I want justice for You in these terrible hours, and You want to get to the cross. Praise You! Thank You for Your restraint. It paved the way for my salvation. ~*Amen*

Remember:

_____

_____

_____

_____

_____

_____

_____

I AM THE CHRIST

Meditation:

"What is it that these men testify against You?"
But He remained silent and made no answer.
Again the high priest asked Him,
"Are you the Christ, the Son of the Blessed?"
And Jesus said, "I am, and you will see
the Son of Man seated at the right hand of Power,
and coming with the clouds of heaven."
And the high priest tore his garments and said,
"What further witnesses do we need?"

~ MARK 14:60-63

"My kingdom is not of this world."
Then Pilate said to Him, "So you are a king?"
Jesus answered, "You say that I am a king.
For this purpose I was born and for this purpose
I have come into the world—to bear witness to
the truth. Everyone who is of the truth listens to
My voice." Pilate said to Him, "What is truth?"
After he had said this, he went back
outside to the Jews and told them,
"I find no guilt in Him."

~ JOHN 18:33-38

(SEE ALSO: MATTHEW 26:57 THRU 27:26; MARK 14:53 THRU 15:15;
LUKE 22:54 THRU 23:25; JOHN 18:12 THRU 19:16)

Reflection:

While Jesus remains silent when wrongly accused, He never misses an opportunity to speak regarding His identity. So when a simple question is put to Him about who He has claimed to be, He answers succinctly and unhesitatingly. In whatever manner He chose to phrase His response in the hours He was being dragged from one trial to another, He makes it known: He is the Son of God, the King of the Jews, whose kingdom is not of this world.

Why remain silent in the face of falsehoods, yet address questions about identity? These confessions of Jesus will seal His fate. Part of the angst of saturating oneself in this narrative is discovering that in these particular hours of inquisition, there is a strong pull to take one's eyes off the mark. Jesus never does. Jesus. Never. Does. He never gets caught up in the frenzy the Jews are creating. He does not get intimidated by Pilate's flexing. He does not weaken through the abuse He is receiving. He is utterly steadfast.

It bears remembering—no one is in charge in these night and morning hours but God. No power is in play that is not subject to the power of God. Pilate suggests otherwise, but Jesus quickly sets him straight: "You would have no authority over me at all unless it had been given you from above" (John 19:11).

What I'm gleaning as I pay attention to how intentional Jesus is with His words is that He is in no way a victim. There is no comparison whatsoever between a powerless victim and the Son of Man, a willing subject of torture and injustice. While my heart aches for the extent of His suffering, it matters that I remember He suffers of His own accord. These atrocities are embraced by Jesus because of the unquenchable love of God for humankind. *That* takes me to my knees!

Response:

Lord Jesus,

You shone so brightly out from among those around You as You were being so terribly mistreated and abused. There are no words for the sacrifice You made in those horrible hours. I am the beneficiary of Your sacrifice. I bow before You now, without an adequate way to thank You. But I love You and I worship You and I praise You for who You are and for the life I have because of what You did for me and for all of humanity. You are "the propitiation for our sins, and not for ours only but also for the sins of the whole world" (1 John 2:2). Thank You, Suffering Savior! ~*Amen*

Remember:

Behold, Your King!

Meditation:

From then on Pilate sought to release Him,
but the Jews cried out, "If you release this man,
you are not Caesar's friend. Everyone who
makes himself a king opposes Caesar."
So when Pilate heard these words, he brought
Jesus out and sat down on the judgment seat at a
place called The Stone Pavement, and in Aramaic
Gabbatha. Now it was the day of Preparation of
the Passover. It was about the sixth hour.
He said to the Jews, "Behold your King!"
They cried out, "Away with Him, away with
Him, crucify Him!" Pilate said to them,
"Shall I crucify your King?" The chief priests
answered, "We have no king but Caesar."
So he delivered Him over to them to be crucified.

~ JOHN 19:12–16

So when Pilate saw that he was gaining
nothing, but rather that a riot was beginning,
he took water and washed his hands before
the crowd, saying, "I am innocent of this man's blood;
see to it yourselves." And all the people answered,
"His blood be on us and on our children!"
Then he released for them Barabbas,
and having scourged Jesus,
delivered Him to be crucified.
Then the soldiers of the governor

took Jesus into the governor's headquarters,
and they gathered the whole battalion before Him.
And they stripped Him and put a scarlet robe on Him,
and twisting together a crown of thorns, they put it
on his head and put a reed in His right hand.
And kneeling before Him, they mocked Him,
saying, "Hail, King of the Jews!" And they spit
on Him and took the reed and struck Him
on the head. And when they had mocked Him,
they stripped Him of the robe and put His own
clothes on Him and led Him away to crucify Him.

~ MATTHEW 27:24–31

Reflection:

Jesus is mocked and tortured by people assuming there is
no possible way He can be who He says He is. I cannot get
the irony of these scenes out of my mind. Here is Jesus,
beaten nearly to death, taunted, spit upon, and endlessly
ridiculed for claiming to be the Son of God and King of the
Jews. His mock-kingly attire makes for the cruelest kind of
make-believe. But the pièce de résistance: "Hail, King of
the Jews!" Mock-worship.

God the Son, presumed to be either a lunatic or a dan-
gerous insurgent, is on display before the crowds and in full
view of God the Father and perhaps even the celestial be-
ings. No one viewing from heaven or earth is on the fence
in these horrible moments. Of course, Pilate's radar is up
for sure, but he is in no way ready to defend Jesus' inno-
cence in the face of the demands of the frenzied crowd. And

there's a big difference between finding Jesus innocent and believing Him to be the Son of God.

As Pilate brings Jesus out before the masses this morning, he presents Him by saying, "Behold, Your King!" Truer words are never spoken. All of Heaven understands precisely who Jesus is. A few believers are likely scattered in the crowd, too, but their voices are never going to be heard above the cries to crucify Jesus. And so the King—the one, true King of Heaven and earth—is given over to be executed, immensely pleasing His enemies.

One day you and I will find this same King coming down from the heavens just as He ascended. I make up in my mind that the Father will say, "Behold, Your King!" and the Church will cry for joy. There will be no mock-worship that day because every knee will be bowed before Him. *All* will know who He truly is!

Response:

Lord Jesus,

How I long for Your return. How I long for the day when the whole earth will understand who You are! And You will finally be worshipped by all humankind, even by those who refuse Your gift of life. I am sorry we mocked You and abused Your body so terribly. I am sorry we would not see You as our King and worship You then. I thank You for the few who did believe and for their faith in the midst of the staunch opposition. I am humbled by their faith in You. Speak to me now, Lord, in these passages that describe what You endured. I ask for this in Your name, Jesus. *~Amen*

Remember:

_____

_____

_____

_____

_____

_____

_____

_____

_____

_____

_____

_____

_____

Do Not Weep for Me

Meditation:

And as they led Him away, they seized one Simon
of Cyrene, who was coming in from the country,
and laid on him the cross, to carry it behind Jesus.
And there followed Him a great multitude of the
people and of women who were mourning and
lamenting for Him. But turning to them Jesus said,
"Daughters of Jerusalem, do not weep for Me,
but weep for yourselves and for your children.
For behold, the days are coming when they will say,
'Blessed are the barren and the wombs that never
bore and the breasts that never nursed!'
Then they will begin to say to the mountains,
'Fall on us,' and to the hills, 'Cover us.'
For if they do these things when the wood is
green, what will happen when it is dry?"

~ LUKE 23:26-31

Reflection:

"Weep for yourselves," says Jesus to those following Him
along the road to Golgotha. These deeply distressed women
catch Jesus' attention and in His grave physical condition,
He pauses to speak to them. Their sorrow is understandably
directed at Jesus, but He needs them to understand it is
misplaced. His chilling, prophetic warning is meant to help
them shift their focus and consider what is actually at stake.

They do not understand. For them, they see a man who was days earlier poised to be their king. He is now nearly unrecognizable as He walks to His death.

But what Jesus is about to do in surrendering His life and then conquering death is going to serve as the sacrifice humanity has been waiting for since we first sinned in the garden of Eden. And yet only a remnant will receive the gift offered to all, and Jesus knows it. Jerusalem's future as a nation is grim, and Jesus knows it. So, for their future and for the future beyond, where men and women will make their choice about what to do with this sacrifice Jesus is about to make, He directs their attention to the real matter at hand.

"If they do these things when the wood is green, what will happen when it is dry?" Jesus is carrying out the will of the Father as He moves toward the cross. At the same time, He is giving them (and us) a look into the soul of humanity. It seems inconceivable that the multitudes stand in the presence of the Messiah and yet are unable or unwilling to believe it is really Him. And Jesus lets them know it's only going to get harder to believe.

Jesus comes to rescue sinners. He comes to give life. While His death is imminent, He is perfectly secure in His own destiny. There is no need for tears for Him. But the future of the multitude following Him is NOT secure, and so our Lord addresses their need. He uses even these arduous moments to try to waken sleeping hearts. The gift of this redirection of attention is as much our gift as it is to those following Jesus through the streets to the site of His execution. He is the Savior. There is no other. Is He yours? He will be if you ask Him!

Response:

Lord Jesus,

Only the Holy Spirit in You could have caused You to be able to think clearly, let alone respond to those grieving for You. Simon was just given Your cross to carry because You could not bear it along the road anymore. But the Spirit WAS alive in You, and so You stopped to make one more passionate plea to those following You on that road. I praise You for Your selflessness. I praise You for showing me what it looks like to love with every breath and every ounce of energy; to love even when you struggle to take another step. Thank You, Jesus! And now, will You take me under the surface so that I learn more deeply about the marvelous words You spoke on the final leg of your walk to the cross? Speak to me, Lord. ~*Amen*

Remember:

_____

_____

_____

_____

_____

_____

_____

Sunday
Day of Rest

THE CRUCIFIXION

Meditation:

So they took Jesus, and He went out,
bearing His own cross, to the place called The Place
of a Skull, which in Aramaic is called Golgotha.
There they crucified Him, and with Him two others
one on either side, and Jesus between them.
Pilate also wrote an inscription and put it on the cross.
It read, "Jesus of Nazareth, the King of the Jews."
Many of the Jews read this inscription, for the
place where Jesus was crucified was near the city,
and it was written in Aramaic, in Latin, and in Greek.
So the chief priests of the Jews said to Pilate,
"Do not write, 'The King of the Jews,' but rather,
'This man said, I am King of the Jews.'" Pilate
answered, "What I have written I have written."
When the soldiers had crucified Jesus, they
took His garments and divided them into four
parts, one part for each soldier; also His tunic.
But the tunic was seamless, woven in one piece
from top to bottom, so they said to one another,
"Let us not tear it, but cast lots for it to see whose
it shall be." This was to fulfill the Scripture which
says, "They divided my garments among them,
and for my clothing they cast lots." So the soldiers
did these things, but standing by the cross of Jesus were
His mother and His mother's sister, Mary the wife
of Clopas, and Mary Magdalene. When Jesus saw
His mother and the disciple whom He loved
standing nearby He said to His mother,

> "Woman, behold, your son!" Then He said to the
> disciple, "Behold, your mother!" And from that
> hour the disciple took her to his own home.
>
> ~ JOHN 19:16–27;
>
> (SEE ALSO: LUKE 23:26–43; MARK 15:21–32; MATTHEW 27:32–44)

Reflection:

John, "the disciple whom He loved" (John 20:2) is recalling what he witnessed at Golgotha. He is the only one to record Jesus' words in this part of our Lord's ordeal, and they are highly personal. Once again, Jesus is the caregiver, knowing what His inner circle's needs are. As He hangs on the cross dying, He sees to it that His mother will be properly cared for. It's a stunning act of other-centeredness, something no ordinary human would be capable of.

Meanwhile the Jewish leaders are straining at gnats about the wording of the sign Pilate has hung over Jesus' head. The soldiers who just crucified Jesus are gambling for His clothing, and passersby jeer as Jesus is suffocating to death. The thieves who hang on either side of Him make their own contribution to the degrading dialogue, but that exchange ends in the salvation of a man's soul, one more act of other-centeredness from Jesus.

There are many silent moments while Jesus hangs suffering—suffocating to death. He is alive upon the cross for about three hours. The words that He says would take only seconds for Him to utter. What of all the rest of these hours? What is our Savior enduring? He confesses feeling forsaken. Physically, He endures a torturous, progressive pain we cannot comprehend. How long do three hours feel to Him?

This is the scene, witnessed by John, of the crucifixion of our Lord. For Jesus, the Son of Man, the final three hours of a thirty-three-year journey end in misery. They also end in victory as He willingly offers up His life as a ransom for many.

Response:

Lord Jesus,

The pain of crucifixion is known to be beyond description. Just the thought of it sends fear into any heart. So, I cannot understand the level of pain You were in let alone how You were able to care for Your mother, for the soldiers who nailed You to the cross, and for the criminal beside You. Praise You for all Your marvelous, sacrificial works in those final moments. I pray You would lead me in my thoughts and feelings as I meditate upon You there, because I have a hard time reconciling the reality that I too was on Your mind that terrible day. How could it be? I fall on my knees before You now. Thank You for my life, my precious suffering Savior! ~Amen

Remember:

_____

_____

_____

_____

_____

All Was Now Finished
the death of Jesus

There will be no reflections added to these passages today. There is no meaningful language that can be added. Read now and meditate as you remember the death of our Savior.

Meditation:

It was now about the sixth hour,
and there was darkness over the whole land
until the ninth hour, while the sun's light failed.
And the curtain of the temple was torn in two.
Then Jesus, calling out with a loud voice, said,
"Father, into your hands I commit my spirit!"
and having said this He breathed His last
Now when the centurion saw what had
taken place, he praised God, saying,
"Certainly this man was innocent!"
And all the crowds that had assembled
for this spectacle, when they saw what had
taken place, returned home beating their breasts.
And all His acquaintances and the women
who had followed Him from Galilee
stood at a distance watching these things.

~ LUKE 23:44–49

And when the sixth hour had come, there was
darkness over the whole land until the ninth hour.
And at the ninth hour Jesus cried with a loud voice,
"Eloi, Eloi, lema sabachthani?" which means,

"My God, my God, why have you forsaken me?"
And some of the bystanders hearing it said,
"Behold, He is calling Elijah." And someone ran
and filled a sponge with sour wine, put it on a reed
and gave it to Him to drink, saying, "Wait, let us see
whether Elijah will come to take Him down."
And Jesus uttered a loud cry and breathed His last.
And the curtain of the temple was torn in two, from top
to bottom. And when the centurion, who stood facing
Him, saw that in this way he breathed His last, he said,
"Truly this man was the Son of God!"

~ MARK 15:33–39

Now from the sixth hour there was darkness over all
the land until the ninth hour. And about the ninth hour
Jesus cried out with a loud voice, saying, "Eli, Eli,
lema sabachthani?" that is, "My God, my God, why
have You forsaken me?" And some of the bystanders,
hearing it, said, "This man is calling Elijah."
And one of them at once ran and took a sponge,
filled it with sour wine, and put it on a reed and
gave it to Him to drink. But the others said, "Wait,
let us see whether Elijah will come to save Him."
And Jesus cried out again with a loud voice
and yielded up His spirit. And behold, the curtain
of the temple was torn in two, from top to bottom.
And the earth shook, and the rocks were split.
The tombs also were opened. And many bodies of
the saints who had fallen asleep were raised,
and coming out of the tombs after his resurrection
they went into the holy city and appeared to many.

When the centurion and those who were with Him,
keeping watch over Jesus, saw the earthquake
and what took place, they were filled with awe
and said, "Truly this was the Son of God!"
There were also many women there,
looking on from a distance, who had followed
Jesus from Galilee, ministering to Him, among whom
were Mary Magdalene and Mary the mother of James
and Joseph and the mother of the sons of Zebedee.

~ MATTHEW 27:45–56

After this, Jesus, knowing that all was now
finished, said (to fulfill the Scripture), "I thirst."
A jar full of sour wine stood there, so they
put a sponge full of the sour wine on a
hyssop branch and held it to His mouth.
When Jesus had received the sour wine,
He said, "It is finished," and He bowed
His head and gave up His spirit.

~ JOHN 19:28–30

Two Days of Silence
DISORIENTATION

Meditation:

> My God, my God, why have you forsaken me?
> Why are you so far from saving me,
>   from the words of my groaning?
> O my God, I cry by day, but you do not
> answer, and by night, but I find no rest.
>
> On you was I cast from my birth, and from
> my mother's womb you have been my God.
> Be not far from me, for trouble is near,
>   and there is none to help.

~ PSALM 22:1–2; 10–11

Reflection:

This Lent we have committed ourselves to being occupied with thoughts of Jesus and who He showed Himself to be in the last days of His earthly life. As we approach the next two entries, we will create space to consider the experience of those who loved Him who are now separated from Him. They spend part of three agonizing days without their Master. We will try to slip into their shoes in some tiny measure.

There is no way to fully understand what Jesus' followers would have been experiencing at the time of His death. Their Beloved had just been savagely tortured and then executed. The psyche's immediate response to trauma is to put a temporary stop on all normal responses and shift into a shutdown mode for self-preservation. So I don't think the extent of their bewilderment can be measured.

Most likely the followers of Jesus are numb. They are in shock, which means their physical bodies, their minds, and their hearts are all affected. The list of symptoms in response to shock is sobering. They cannot possibly process because they are frozen in a state of disorientation. Their minds are likely darting from one scene to another, trying to find some footing that will steady them. They are without Jesus. They are individually and collectively without Him.

Let's spend today in a posture of inward silence. Let's try to enter that space of numbness with those who followed Him. Let's ask the Holy Spirit if He might give us a glimpse into what they felt so that we might better appreciate what our brothers and sisters endured. Moreover, let's use today as a launch pad for praise because we will never have to experience the pain of separation from our Lord!

Response:

Lord Jesus,

Today I ponder what it could have felt like to have You ripped away, to know that You died. I cannot imagine. This was a terrible weight your followers had to bear. You would not leave them in this disorientation for long, but the hours and days must have felt endless and excruciating to them. What would You have me understand about these days of silence and separation? Please speak to me. Please give me understanding so that I more deeply appreciate the gift of Your life in me and Your presence with me! I know I take that for granted. Praise you, Jesus! ~*Amen*

Remember:

_____

_____

_____

_____

_____

_____

_____

_____

_____

Two Days of Silence
DEVASTATION

Meditation:

"Truly, truly I say to you, you will weep
and lament, but the world will rejoice."

~ JOHN 16:20

For my sighing comes instead of my bread,
and my groanings are poured out like water.
For the thing that I fear comes upon me,
and what I dread befalls me.

~ JOB 3:23–25

The Spirit himself intercedes for us
with groanings too deep for words.

~ ROMANS 8:26

Reflection:

When the dark moments of disorientation lift for the followers of Jesus, devastation will take its place. It's a terrible
thing to have your feet finally land and discover you are
in the nightmare you feared you might be in. But this is
reality for Jesus' companions. The thing that takes their
experience even further out of the known stratosphere is
this: Jesus wasn't just their beloved companion and teacher.
He was the one who was going to save them. He was the
Christ, the Messiah. He was the Son of God. He was their

future hope—and He is dead. They are grappling with the dismantling of their entire lives.

Many of them are also grappling with their abandonment of Jesus. They are likely wracked with guilt, having done the very thing they pledged never to do; in fact, what they believed they were incapable of doing. And Jesus is not there for them to make amends. They cannot ask for forgiveness.

Fear of exposure and persecution also grips those left behind. They hunker down together, trying to stay off the Jewish leaders' grid. This adds yet another complicated, significant layer of stress. This is just a paralyzing, anxiety laden time for them. Honestly, Jesus was so detailed trying to prepare them for His absence, but it doesn't appear as though much of it is able to come to bear for the disciples and others.

A few of Jesus' followers, mainly the women, are able to make themselves useful by preparing Jesus' body for burial and taking care of burial details. That might be a helpful "if temporary" distraction. But the majority are left to do nothing but wait (in hiding) and pray that the cloud of disorientation and devastation will mercifully dissipate.

There is not another time in all of history like these few days. And there will never be a time like it again. For two nights and part of three days, one of the members of the Trinity is dead. The world is without God the Son.

Response:

Lord Jesus,

Even as Your Spirit takes me back to those terrible days, I grieve Your death. The idea that one could be without You for a moment, let alone three interminable days, is beyond my comprehension. I know the Father sustained Your devastated followers during that time, though I doubt they would have been able to feel it if at all. What would You have me understand as I sit in these days of silence? Speak to me, Lord, and teach me. I praise You and I worship You!

~*Amen*

Remember:

_____

_____

_____

_____

_____

_____

_____

_____

He Has Risen
From the Dead!

Meditation:

Now after the Sabbath, toward the dawn of the
first day of the week, Mary Magdalene and the other
Mary went to see the tomb. And behold, there
was a great earthquake, for an angel of the Lord
descended from heaven and came and rolled back
the stone and sat on it. His appearance was like
lightning, and his clothing white as snow.
And for fear of him the guards trembled
and became like dead men. But the angel said
to the women, "Do not be afraid, for I know
that you seek Jesus who was crucified.
He is not here, for He has risen, as He said.
Come, see the place where He lay. Then go quickly
and tell His disciples that He has risen from the dead,
and behold, He is going before you to Galilee;
there you will see Him. See, I have told you."
So they departed quickly from the tomb with fear
and great joy, and ran to tell his disciples.

~ MATTHEW 28:1–8

(SEE ALSO: MARK 16:1–8; LUKE 24:1–12; JOHN 20:1–18;

1 CORINTHIANS 15:1–8)

Reflection:

The event of Jesus' resurrection involved more people than
we might think. It all begins a little before first light on the

third day after His death. The soldiers guarding the tomb, several different women, Jesus' disciples, and a few other favored ones are invited into the first hours of the greatest, most significant miracle in history. The tomb is empty and Jesus is alive!

Fear, great joy, trembling, astonishment, weeping—all are experienced by various ones depending on how and when they arrive on the scene. Some feel an earthquake, some witness an angel rolling the stone away. Some are spoken to by an angel. All are dumbfounded to find Jesus missing from the grave where they had personally laid Him.

A whole new wave of disorientation launches. This new news is equally as disorienting as Jesus' death had been. How could it be otherwise! They have grappled for a few days with the crippling reality of Jesus' death. Now their reality is called into question again with news that the impossible has just taken place!

Those whose memories fail them have the words of an angel to remind them what Jesus had already told them. He is risen from the dead! Still, this is something no natural mind has the capacity to assimilate. Before too long, however, Jesus will show Himself to His beloved ones, and they will know because they will see! He is risen!

Response:

Oh Lord Jesus,

How relieved I am to be at this part of the story! Hallelujah! Hallelujah, my Jesus! You rose from the dead, just as You said You would! Praise You, Risen Savior! The days

of mourning felt as though they would never end and, of course, Your followers were not sure they would. I would have been just like them. I would have thought You were really gone, that I was parted from You for good. But that is NOT what happened! You rose again! You defeated death! You purchased the redemption of anyone who would believe what You did and make You their Lord! You did that for me! Thank You! Thank You! Praise You! Death could not hold You! I bow before You, Jesus, my Risen Lord!
~*Amen*

Remember:

_____

_____

_____

_____

_____

_____

_____

_____

_____

Entering His Glory

Meditation:

"Did not the Messiah have to suffer
these things and then enter His glory?"
Beginning with Moses and all the Prophets,
He explained to them what was said
in all the Scriptures concerning Himself.

~ LUKE 24:26-27

For God so loved the world,
that He gave His one and only Son
that whoever believes in Him
shall not perish but have eternal life.

~ JOHN 3:16

(SEE ALSO: MATTHEW 28:9-20; LUKE 24:13-53; JOHN 20:17 - 21:25)

Reflection:

Tomorrow we celebrate the resurrection of our Lord! I cannot thank you enough for traveling with me these many weeks and being willing to linger in the details of the events leading up to and through Jesus' death and resurrection. This has been an experience for me unlike any other, and I'm so grateful to God for the way He has met with me. I pray you are, too!

It's one thing to think back upon events that took place over two thousand years ago, and an altogether other thing to be so immersed in the story that the news of Jesus' resurrection hits you with a sense of disbelief and wonder as it might have if you were there to witness it! That is where I find myself as I write.

I have a deeper appreciation for the immeasurable power of God that not only sustained Jesus through the horror of His last days, but defeated death by raising Him back to life! And why did God make this wondrous and terrible sacrifice? LOVE. Love drove the creation of and execution of the plan of redemption for humanity! GOD IS LOVE. What else *would* He do to reconcile souls to Himself? He was simply being Himself, eager to pay for my sins, willing to do for me what I had no power to do for myself.

Jesus, the Lamb of God who "takes away the sin of the world" (John 1:29), was and is the essence of love and graciousness and passion and truth. He is the sole One who defines sacrifice, sinlessness, and other-centeredness. All the beautiful gifts I have because I belong to Him are mine because *HE* is mine! Can you fathom having Jesus Christ as your chief companion? I can hardly contain myself!

And so I worship! I ascribe worth to my magnificent Lord, seated now at the right hand of God the Father (Acts 2:33)! All glory is His. He has entered His glory, and I have the honor of making much of Him! What a gift! I bow at His feet and pay homage to the One who gave everything to save me! I have done precisely NOTHING to earn or deserve Him, and, yet, because of who *HE* is, I am His and He is mine (Song of Songs 2:16)!

Let praise abound, brothers and sisters! We are children of the Risen King of Glory!

He is risen! He is risen indeed!

Happy Easter ~

Response:

Lord Jesus,

How I love You! I simply cannot believe I am Yours! YOURS! You are more beautiful to me than ever after traveling with You these many weeks leading up to this glorious day. I give You praise, my King! I worship You, Lord of heaven and earth, the One by whom and for whom all things were made! All that I am and have is Yours, so even my praise and worship is a regifting to You. I am so happy I can worship You! You are the risen Lord—MY risen Lord! Thank You, from my soul, for all You did to ransom me. Thank You, from my soul, for making me Yours. Thank You for all that awaits all of us who belong to You! Tomorrow is Easter! I celebrate You, Your victory over death, and the life I have in You! All my Hope is in You, Risen Lord.

I pray this in Your name—the name of the resurrected Christ! ~*Amen and Amen.*

Remember:

_____

_____

_____

_____

_____

_____

Anne Barbour

Aɴɴᴇ Bᴀʀʙᴏᴜʀ has been a guest speaker in both church and conference settings all over the nation including the Billy Graham Schools of Evangelism, The Billy Graham Training Center, and various women's conferences.

Her first book entitled, *The Savior Has Come | An Advent Devotional*, was released in the Fall of 2020. Anne also writes a wide range of conference material that help women find and maintain a core connect with God so that He might do in and through them all that He intends. And she maintains a blog she describes as "musings and mutterings" about walking with God.

Anne has also been active in the arena of contemporary worship as a singer and songwriter for 37 years. She was a founding member of the Maranatha Praise Band, now the Tommy Coomes Band, and has traveled the world leading worship on platforms for Billy Graham, Franklin Graham, Chosen Women, Harvest Crusades, Anne Graham Lotz, Jill Briscoe, and many others. She has developed and led workshops on worship and songwriting throughout the country as part of the Tommy Coomes Band.

Anne and her husband John travel extensively leading worship and ministering in churches and conference centers. They have recorded seven CD's of their own and have fifteen as part of the Tommy Coomes Band. Anne has a solo project entitled, "The Story of Perfect Love," designed as a catalyst for personal worship. Anne has also been a studio musician for the past 30 years recording for television, radio, and various recording artists.

Anne and her husband, John, have one amazing son, along with his beautiful bride, and their grand-puppy. They live in Newbury Park, California.

For information about Anne's blog, bookings, and product visit:

annebarbour.com

Offering Thanks to the Risen Savior

The following pages are for you to either write or draw on. What could you offer Jesus through words or pictures that would express your gratitude to Him? Jesus offered His life as His expression of love for you. Ask the Holy Spirit to help you creatively offer your thanks.

Let them thank the Lord for His steadfast love,
for His wondrous works to the children of man!

~ PSALM 107:21